Princess in Overalls

Princess in Overalls

A book on littleness, miracles and the power of prayer.

All Bible quotations are from the New American Bible.

Printed in the United States of America
First Printing, 2011
ISBN 978-0-9865601-0-1

To my real-life, flesh-and-bone prince—Arda—who is, along with my mom and dad my greatest blessing and my most precious gift from God. Thank you for loving me, and for always finding a way to love me more! Thank you for supporting me and making me write this book. You believed in me. You made it all happen! I love you, my little one.

To my parents, Vilma and Fernando, who made me who I am, and to whom I owe everything. My love for you is unending!

To Hannah, Daniela, and Tomas my gifts from God, our most awesome miracles, I dreamed of you before you ever existed. I love you today, always and forever, and I praise God for you!

To Tita and Tico, for being like storybook grandparents – simply wonderful.

And to You, Jesus, You who have sheltered me, loved me and guided me. You have been a constant presence in my life. You have showered me with blessings. I dedicate my work to You because without You in my life, there would have never been a "Princess in Overalls"!

Contents

Princess in Overalls

Foreword

It is rare to find a book that combines the refreshing vision of children and the rich wisdom that comes from experience with life. *Princess in Overalls* combines both. On the one hand, we meet Ellie, the "princess" as she grows from child to mature adult. On the other hand, we meet Carolina Prada, the author, who captures profound lessons from the events in Ellie's life. We also meet important figures in Ellie's life, her parents Reuben and Anna, and those who entered her life as the years went by.

Ellie receives many lessons from her parents, lessons structured to her age and experience. These lessons form, as it were, the basic truths about life that a child and adolescent need to learn. Carolina then uses these lessons to examine issues important for everyone of whatever age. Most importantly, she presents these lessons from a Christian point of view. Then, in each case, she quotes passages from Scripture to support and to enrich what she has to say.

What does Ellie need to learn as she grows up? So many things! What is fear and how should we conquer it? How do we relate to others our own age? How do we relate to those older than we? How do we react when we encounter people who are unkind and mean? What dreams shall we form for our future? How do we know what our role in life is going to be? What do we do in the face of disappointment? How do we foster relationships? How do we face the end of relationships? How can we recognize that someone is the person we would like to marry? How do we forgive injuries done to us?

Ellie receives answers to these questions and more. Carolina moves us beyond a child's perspective for these questions. She takes us to a deep level and helps us to see what path will bring us the peace and joy that God wishes us to experience during our lives. She shows us how close God is to us at each moment and how God loves us. She also shows how he longs to help us and how he guides us along our way. We human beings live in a divine milieu: God is with us.

This book might be called one of "self-help." But a much better description would be: one of divine help. Carolina shows us that it is by the free gift of grace given to us in Jesus Christ that we can move beyond the self and act in a truly Christian way. She guides us to see that Christian courage requires us to be kind, gentle, tenderhearted, and compassionate. She shows that the highest of the Christian values, love, is something far greater and far more challenging than any feeling. Love is a choice made again and again, both when it is easy to love and when it is hard to love. Love constantly offers a challenge to rise above the purely natural, to rise above our instinctive reactions, and to make our response one of kindness and mercy. Carolina shows that to be a Christian is to be someone of courage and valor, someone who insists on the highest level of human behavior, and someone who can envision dreams that become a reality.

This book is a treasure of wisdom for both young and old. In it readers will find many echoes of events in their own lives. They will receive guidance on how to prove worthy of the name of Christian. And they will learn, in their treatment of others, to show the compassionate and loving face of Jesus Christ.

Dr. Shirley Sullivan, FRSC
Professor Emeritus of Classics
University of British Columbia

Princess in Overalls

The Fire

–1–

Ellie had enormous blue eyes of immeasurable beauty. Her pink cheeks and baby blues were framed by soft brown hair. She was the youngest in her family, the fifth one, to be exact, among a group of older children, her "big" brothers and sisters. She was—the baby. Ellie was not only the baby of the family; she was also a miracle, whose life continued within the most uncertain of circumstances. Yes, a miracle, a special girl for whom God had great plans.

One night, Ellie could not sleep, because, as usual, she was scared. She did not like having to go to sleep all by herself. But her mother had said she was a big girl now and had told her how big girls go to sleep on their own. She was "OK" with the idea of going to bed by herself, and she was pretty sure she could fall soundly asleep on her own, if only…if only she didn't have to turn the lights off! She had already put on her cozy pajamas, and now she gave some thought to a solution for her problem—how to go to bed in a room that was not pitch black.

After giving some careful consideration to all her options, she came up with what she thought was the best solution. She decided to take the bedside lamp with her under the covers! Her logic was that, in this way, darkness would give way to light. All the while, her parents would think she was asleep. "Who can see the light of a table lamp if it is under the covers?" she asked herself. "Nobody!" she happily answered in the blink of an eye. Good thinking! Or at least it seemed that way…

It was like being in a camping tent, and she was loving every minute of it. She had placed her favorite stuffed animals, a pink bunny and a white duck, right next to her, and now she was ready to go to sleep. Everything was just perfect. Yes, she felt safe now, and her eyes felt heavier and heavier as she gave in to a deep sleep.

Ellie was somewhere high up in the sky. She felt like a butterfly moving in an effortless exchange between flying and floating. She was not sure where she was, just that it was a majestic place somewhere amidst the clouds. She was not sure how long she had been there, but it didn't matter anyway since she was in such bliss! It was a moment of sheer happiness and peace. Ellie was in a place that was so wonderful and so beautiful that it felt like home.

All of a sudden, she started falling at a very high speed, tumbling down fast, as if from the sky. She could feel butterflies in her stomach. Suddenly, she felt as if she had dropped heavily onto the bed, like a sack of potatoes. It was not the first time she had had this experience; it had happened quite a few times before. She could not visit this special place whenever she wanted; it just happened inadvertently every now and then. Was that wonderful place real? Did it really happen that she went there? Where had she been? Was that just what big people call a dream?

When she opened her eyes, there was a big commotion in her room…huge, engulfing flames were surrounding her. It turned out that the light bulb from the table lamp had started a fire as it rested on the bed covers. Her bed was on fire, and she could feel a tremendous heat on her soft baby skin; it felt as if a thousand pins were pressing against her cheeks. Suddenly, like a miracle, she saw a pair of huge hands coming toward her. They were the hands of her father, Reuben, that man she adored. He picked her up and held her safely in his arms.

Perplexed and speechless, her parents, Anna and Reuben, could see the whole mattress completely scorched—that is, the entire mattress except for a circle with a circumference just big enough to accommodate Ellie and her stuffed animals. Horrible thoughts dashed through their minds—their baby girl could have been badly burnt or could even have died. Anna and Reuben felt a mixture of the deepest gratefulness, relief and, at the same time, horror. In bewilderment, they wondered if this enigma would ever be explained.

But sometimes things just happen, and there is just no way to explain them! Sometimes things happen in a certain way, not because we deserve them or because we have asked for them—we certainly did not expect them—they are just gifts that happen in our lives. Anna and Reuben looked at their little girl as she cuddled between them and felt immensely thankful. Ellie never fully understood what had happened—though her parents made sure she learned that a lamp under the bed covers was just not a good idea.

Ellie was four years old.

Let's be little!

Isn't it a mystery how "little ones" live in a mix between reality and fantasy; never truly sure of what is real? They dream so intensely that when they wake up, they bounce around in joy, trying to replay every detail of their dream. They are convinced that, in fact, they lived through whatever experience they had. These "little ones" are positive that the daydream, vision, illusion or mirage actually happened. I can't help but wonder...are these experiences real? Are "little ones" somehow able to actually go to these magical places? Do their imaginary friends really exist? Do angels really come and play with them? Can they see things we don't? Who are we to say no?

After all, it has been so long since we ourselves were "little ones" that maybe our perceptions have changed. We are so certain of what the limits are that we do not allow room for the unexplained. Our minds quickly disregard our experiences as a dream due to something we ate, or as something for our psychiatrist to explain as coming – because of too much stress.

Our awareness of the extraordinary often fades away as we get older. Maybe because it is then that we start learning about our limits, about what is possible and what is impossible. For the "little ones," there are no limits to what is possible, only undiscovered frontiers to which they are determined to go. And it is this determination that makes all the difference.

So let's think for a moment: What if "little ones" have a way of entering different "dimensions"? What if they are able to experience a multitude of worlds, being here and there as they please? We should not be afraid of this possibility. After all, "little ones" are not fully here yet.

By this, what I mean is that "little ones" are like heavenly beings for whom nothing is impossible. They seem to fluctuate between heaven and earth—maybe because when we are little, we have an easier time keeping a strong connection to the heavenly realm and to the unknown dimensions of God's created universe.

I deeply believe that we should not tuck away the "little one" in us. Why do we have to stop being "little" on the inside? As we grow up, our body changes and ages, we gain knowledge, we become wiser (hopefully!). But the fact that our body and intellect can and will grow does not mean that we must sacrifice the "little one" that we once were. We are all "little ones" deep inside. The problem is that some of us hide that part of us in a deep dark corner and suppress it. Some of us have almost forgotten how to get in touch with that part of ourselves. Nevertheless, this does not mean that it is an impossible thing to do. All we need in order to get in touch with it is to have the will to do it. We all have been "little" before, so if we allow ourselves to regain contact with the "little one" we once were, we will be free to fully enjoy all the things God intends us to enjoy and to experience all that He has in store for us.

You must be wondering what I mean by "little." Well, what I mean by "little" is the person, big or small, who:

- *Is keeping alive that side of himself/herself that knows how to trust and love completely...both the people in their lives and God our Father.*
- *Does not know ego and does not know how to fake emotions—what you see is what you get!*
- *Is always willing to learn more.*
- *Finds joy in simple moments.*
- *Is not afraid to love.*
- *Is eternally seeking and searching for happiness.*
- *Is not limited by anything and is not afraid to dream.*

If we give value to that side of us, we will have much richer experiences, and we will be able to stay more easily connected to the heavenly realm. We surely will be connected to God our Father by always believing, hoping, enjoying, trusting and allowing ourselves to have a perfect balance between our mind, our body, our heart and our soul—a good balance between our humanity and our spirituality. When we maintain the connection to our heavenly Father, we can enrich our lives and those of others by shining on them the graces that we receive, sharing the love and the peace that light up our lives. Let's allow our "littleness" to surface and take over our hearts!

Wisdom to contemplate:

"At that time the disciples approached Jesus and said, 'Who is the greatest in the kingdom of heaven?' He called a child over, placed it in their midst, and said, 'Amen, I say to you, unless you turn and become like children, you will not enter the kingdom of heaven. Whoever humbles himself like this child is the greatest in the kingdom of heaven.'" (Mathew 18:1-5)

"Let the children come to me; do not prevent them, for the kingdom of God belongs to such as these. Amen, I say to you, whoever does not accept the kingdom of God like a child will not enter it." (Mark 10:14-15)

"Amen, I say to you, whoever does not accept the kingdom of God like a child will not enter it." (Luke 18:17)

The Miracle

-2-

Anna always recounted to Ellie how different she was from the first moment she saw her. With the other children, there had been nothing unusual. At the moment the nurses placed them in her arms in the delivery room, like most babies, they had their eyes tightly closed, were crying and had red, wrinkled faces. But when the nurse brought Ellie to her mother's arms, her eyes were wide open, and she lovingly looked at her mom.

From the first moment Anna saw her, Ellie was gleaming as if illuminated by an invisible spotlight. She glowed with a luminous shine that was almost imperceptible yet still there. From the very first day, she was unique. That little baby girl radiated a peace and a serenity that was hard to describe. Her peacefulness and calmness communicated a sort of perfect conformity with her new situation. Yes indeed, from the very first moment, her big blue eyes were already open, looking around as if she was trying to learn all about her surroundings, delighted to be alive, enjoying every minute.

This baby had a purpose for coming uninvited. Her determination to be part of this aching family had made it clear that from that moment on everything would be different, very different indeed. As she looked at her daughter's face, Anna saw how God had blessed her family, and she rejoiced, knowing deep in her heart that everything would be just fine.

You see, Ellie had been a surprise. "Well, it is a fact. Congratulations, Anna. You are pregnant!" the doctor had said. "It is impossible. Look…I am sure, so please have the test done again," Anna had answered adamantly. She had gotten into her car and driven home free of worries. After all, as she had said, she had been sure she was not expecting another child.

A second time, she had found herself at the doctor's office, and for the second time the doctor had said, "Well, Anna, as I said, the test is positive. Congratulations!" By now, she was getting irritated. "Couldn't the doctor do his job right? she had thought angrily. "Oh, for goodness' sake! After all, this is what he does for a living!"

Anna had not believed the doctor when he had told her she was expecting yet another child. She had been so insistent she was not pregnant that she had had him repeat the test three times before she finally assimilated the fact that it was not a mistake.

There was a baby coming, but how? She had been so careful! So many things went through Anna's mind. So many fears were haunting her. This was far from the ideal time to have a baby. Reuben and Anna were on the brink of a separation. Reuben seemed to have fallen out of love; he was cold and distant and showed no interest in making things better.

What a trial this would be. What was she going to do? By now, she had tried everything to save her marriage, without a shred of success. She desperately needed the situation to change, but how? Lately she had been so brokenhearted that she barely found the strength to get up every morning and face the day. How was she going to take care of this new baby? She felt so lonely.

When Anna got married, she was only eighteen. She had been going steady with Reuben since she was fifteen. She was thirty-one now, a woman and a mother. He was the only man she had ever known. Anna's life had always been about her family. Her first baby came when she was nineteen years old, when she was a child herself. As devoted Catholics, they were open to life, and children came in sequence about every two years. When she got the news about her new pregnancy, the youngest of her other children, Anthony, was six.

She had always made an effort to have a happy family. She felt a boundless love for each and every one of her children. To her, each and every one of them was precious; motherhood was a real joy for her. She had had no doubt Reuben was the love of her life, the father of her children, the man she was born to be with. It was unfathomable to think about her life without him. But he had changed, and the change had been going on for a long time now. Only a miracle could save her marriage and restore their love.

We must do our part

In life, when we go through trials, often we pray. But often we pray with doubt and fear in our heart. These things are the opposite of faith. How can a prayer without faith be effective? When we pray, we must pray with confidence—and know that prayers are always heard.

If the answer that comes back is different from what we expected, it does not mean it is not the right one; it only means that there was a better solution to our problem. It is important for us to give the benefit of the doubt, to recognize the fact that we might not always know what the best outcome for a situation is. After all, there is a chance that there can be moments in our life when we might not know the best road to follow. We should not be stubborn, obstinate or inflexible, stuck to a specific idea. We need to trust and be aware of the fact that everything is perfect because God is in charge of our lives.

We must let things flow, with the certainty that in the process we are learning and growing. We must be confident that our prayers are being heard by a loving Father who would never ignore us and who has promised to give good things to those who ask. He reminds us in Holy Scripture: Would we ever ignore the request of one of our children? Now, if we, who have so many faults and defects, are not able to deny our kids anything, then what are the chances that He will ignore our requests? Think about how God is perfect; He is love Himself. Now think about how He has made us, His children. Think about all His promises and about His amazing love. It is simply impossible that He would ignore our prayers.

Therefore, we need to make sure that we understand and know in our hearts that even though at times it might take longer than expected, and even though from time to time our need might be met in a way less than hoped for or anticipated, our prayers are always answered. When we ask for help, we must do it with the absolute certainty that help will come, and we must know that invariably all things will come to us, with our welfare as a first priority.

Jesus said, "Ask and you will receive; seek and you will find; knock and the door will be opened to you." (Luke 11:9) If we pay attention to this scripture verse, we will realize that it requires action on our part. We cannot just pray for something to happen. We cannot just wish things were different. We cannot just sit and hope for something to happen. We need to contribute to the miracles in our lives by asking, seeking and knocking. We need to try our best to make things happen. We must take an active role in our lives and be participants in the miracles that we will experience.

We cannot just passively sit and wait and complain about how we pray and pray and hope and hope and nothing changes. We need to be more involved and take responsibility for the direction our life is going. And we must know that through prayer that direction can always change. It is up to us; it is up to God. Let's learn how to pray and work on improving our relationship with God. Let's strengthen our faith and work hard at doing our part. And, as St. Paul advises in Romans 8, let's hope and eagerly wait with perseverance for the best to happen. I guarantee you that then we can never be disappointed, because hope in God does not disappoint.

Wisdom to contemplate:

"Learn to savor how good the LORD is; happy are those who take refuge in him." (Psalm 34:9)

"If you have faith the size of a mustard seed, you will say to this mountain, 'Move from here to there,' and it will move. Nothing will be impossible for you." (Matthew 17:20)

"For in hope we were saved. Now hope that sees for itself is not hope. For who hopes for what one sees? But if we hope for what we do not see, we wait with endurance....We know that all things work for good for those who love God, who are called according to his purpose." (Romans 8:24-25,28)

"Hope does not disappoint, because the love of God has been poured out into our hearts through the Holy Spirit that has been given to us." (Romans 5:5)

"Faith is the realization of what is hoped for and evidence of things not seen." (Hebrews 11:1)

Prayer Answered

–3–

A miracle! Wasn't that exactly what happened? After all, from the moment Reuben found out about the pregnancy, he was transformed. He assured Anna everything would be different. All he wanted was a new opportunity to make everything right. Anna did not need much convincing; she was overjoyed about his new disposition. What a transformation! She knew this was the change she had been praying for. She was certain that their love deserved another chance.

Indeed, Reuben was a new man. He had made a huge mistake and so he was determined to clear the past, salvage their marriage and recover their love. He was like a completely different person, determined not to waste this chance. He made the necessary arrangements to move to a new city in order to start a brand new life. He decided to look for a new job, and he found one. He had no doubt in his mind that this job was the first step toward redemption. It represented a fresh start.

Reuben knew that to secure happiness, they would have to leave the past where it belongs—in the past. He did not want the old memories lingering in the present, eroding their relationship and threatening their future. Reuben knew that in order for them to have a shot at happiness, together as a family, a new life had to start. They would never look back.

Reuben was a completely changed person. He found himself crazy head-over-heels in love with his new baby girl, Ellie, the miracle in their lives. Somehow the news of this unplanned baby had touched him deeply inside. He dedicated himself to his family and spent every minute of his life giving love to his children and his new baby girl. He vowed to himself to never hurt Anna again, and he never did; after all, she was the love of his life.

For Anna, Reuben's reaction when he first heard the news of the new pregnancy had been a mystery. She had been sure he would explode, be irate at the fact that somehow an undesirable "accident" had happened. Astonished, she heard him talk about a second chance. A second chance was all she had been praying for, a second chance for their family to have a future together, for their love to flourish again. "Thank you, God, for you have rescued our love when it was hopeless. You have made possible the impossible," she prayed. She was in awe of God's goodness and faithfulness. She was full of gratitude and amazed at the power of prayer. She smiled as she pondered the glorious truth that, as Holy Scripture says, nothing is impossible for those who trust in the Lord.

The power of prayer

Yes...the answer to a prayer sometimes comes in disguise, but it always comes. And when it comes, we must learn to acknowledge it and be grateful. It is easy to remember God when we are going through a hardship; then we approach Him and intensely ask for help. But when things are good, we tend to forget to thank Him. Oftentimes we forget that gratefulness is important, and we end up not giving the glory and praise that is due to God. To remember to say thank you is important, because in doing so, we make ourselves aware of the gifts that are constantly given to us, we feel blessed, and we truly understand God's awesome love for us.

Let's pray, so that:

- *We can be less selfish, desiring to be givers instead of receivers: We must get rid of "I want! I expect! I deserve!" and think "What can I give both to others and to God?" After all Scripture says that it is more blessed to give than to receive! Now many times when we think about giving, we think in terms of giving money. But sometimes the most precious thing that we can give or share is not material. Oftentimes what is most valuable for us is in fact what is most precious for us to give. For example, we can share a friend. Let's have a desire to share those special people who have come into our lives, so that they may go and touch others in the same way that they have come into our lives and touched us!*

➢ *<u>We can find joy in every situation:</u> "Consider it all joy, my brothers, when you encounter various trials, for you know that the testing of your faith produces perseverance" (James 1:2-3). Mother Teresa used to say, "The best way to show our gratitude is to accept everything with joy". And that "a joyful heart is the result of a heart burning with love". We may not always be able to give much, but we can all always give the joy that springs from a heart that is in love with God. Let's give thanks for all that we have, and have had! Let's give our best to God—a heart full of joy!*

➢ *<u>We are not proud and we can surrender totally to the will of God:</u> "Your will be done" (Matthew 6:10). We pray this constantly, but when it is time to apply it to real life events, we have a hard time accepting it. Many times, we want our way, we want what we want, we get upset if we don't get it, and we cannot even find a reason to be grateful. The fact is that we deserve nothing. We cannot allow ourselves to be disheartened by anything, not even when at first sight it seems that our prayers have not been answered. Mother Teresa also used to say, "If we are discouraged, it is a sign of pride. We must not let anything disturb us so much and fill us with so much sorrow or discouragement that it makes us forfeit the joy of serving God and thanking God in all that happens in our lives!" In Holy*

Scripture God reminds us to "Persevere in prayer, being watchful in it with thanksgiving" (Colossians 4:2). As we turn to Him and to His love, we can face everything with an attitude of loving trust. A song I love says: "Jesus knows the heartache that you are feeling deep inside...and He will heal your heart!" So even when it seems impossible to remain cheerful and we barely have the strength to smile, we can draw our strength from Him who is always there for us. Him, who is our rock and our salvation.

If we do not make prayer and thanksgiving a habit, inadvertently we will have a tendency to become unaware of our blessings. On the other hand, when we are grateful, we feel closer to Him and we become happy as we ponder how blessed we are. Being happy is easy when we understand how much love is constantly being poured our way. The ability to understand this is a grace given by God, and God always gives good things to those who ask.

If we just have a little faith, if we trust a little more, if we are just a bit more grateful, we will be aware of all the miracles that happen in our lives. And we will take pleasure in the fact that we have come to know and understand that God is a reality and not a myth. We will feel God, alive in our heart, not just as words in a book we hardly ever read. He will bless us with the desire to get to know Him more through the power of His holy Word. We will marvel at the fact that He is living inside us, guiding us and providing strength to us in every situation, so that we may reflect His love to others. We will be able to console because He has given us consolation; we will be able to love because He has given us love. Then we will be examples and living proof of the miracles that He performs in our lives.

Wisdom to contemplate:

"Everything is possible to one who has faith." (Mark 9:23)

"Therefore I tell you, all that you ask for in prayer, believe that you will receive it and it shall be yours." (Mark 11:24)

"Rejoice always. Pray without ceasing. In all circumstances give thanks, for this is the will of God for you in Christ Jesus." (1 Thessalonians 5:16-18)

"O LORD of hosts, happy are those who trust in you!" (Psalm 84:13)

Happiness
–4–

Ellie never really cried. Beaming with happiness, she was always smiling. As she got older, she became the sweetest little girl. Everybody who met her would fall in love with her right away.

"Why is it that all the people who pass by, even when they are strangers, stop and smile at me and say nice things?" she asked her parents.

"It is because you are a princess, Ellie," Anna answered lovingly.

"Hmm…a princess," she thought. "I like that!" She never doubted this; after all, she was convinced her parents only spoke the truth! In any event, she loved the idea of being a princess, and the explanation made sense to her.

Ellie's memories of her early childhood were all, without exception, happy ones—her parents adored her and made her feel safe. Her brothers and sisters were often not home, but when they were, they were funny and made her laugh.

One day, the electricity went out, and while they were waiting for it to come back, they played with the candle wax that melts as the candles burn. They were pouring hot wax onto their hands, testing who could take the most heat.

"Ellie cannot play. After all, I am sure she cannot take the pain and will cry like a baby!" said one of her older brothers, with a touch of malice and a grin in his face.

"I can do it. I won't cry," said Ellie, determined to take any kind of pain in order to show them she was part of the gang!

They looked at each other and then at Anna, who gave them a look they understood very well. "OK, Ellie, you can join us," said the oldest brother.

She had been able to become part of the competition, and she was not about to give up. This was her chance to show them she was not a baby anymore. When the hot wax first touched her small, soft hand, her eyes filled with tears, but she managed not to cry. For her, this was like an initiation into the next stage of her life.

She enjoyed the jokes and games they played that night. When the lights came back on, her older brother was standing on his head, inventing faces that made everybody laugh. "Without a doubt," she thought to herself, "this has been the best night of my life!"

Happiness is at hand

Isn't it wonderful to be able to find happiness in such simple adventures? I am amazed at how much happiness "little ones" can enjoy just because they want to. Wouldn't it be fantastic if we, too, could find happiness in the simple, sweet moments of our lives? Wouldn't it be great if, like "little ones," we were able to seek the sweet juice of life without allowing trivial things to get in the way? Wouldn't it be just perfect if we could stop and make an effort, even if for a minute, to detach ourselves from problems and from the monotony of the everyday and aim for the extraordinary? I am convinced that half of our problems would go away if only we were able to surrender to the beauty of being alive and being loved by God. Yes, let's pause for breath and think about all the reasons why we can be happy, instead of all the reasons why we think we are unhappy.

If we just took the time to smile and delight in a simple moment of joy, then we would be able to see that it is in the little things that happiness is hiding. It is in the ability to appreciate the everyday things that we start feeling tranquility and joy. Why is it that we are never satisfied with our situation? Why is it that once we achieve one of our goals, we immediately ignore what has been achieved and set our eyes on the next thing? Some of us are just never satisfied, always

desiring what we do not have, and this is truly sad. If we only could find happiness in the small things that make our lives unique, then happiness would be in our hearts most of the time. We must stop ourselves if we find ourselves complaining about our circumstances. We must try to wake up asking ourselves, "What am I grateful for? What am I blessed to have? Who loves me? Whom do I love? What am I going to enjoy today?" In this way, we will be preparing ourselves to have a great day.[1]

If we are willing to be like "little ones," then, like them, we will find a million reasons to be happy and a million things worth enjoying. Big moments in our lives fly by, leaving us only memories. But simple, small reasons to be happy are waiting for us every day! If we can learn to find joy in these little things, and use our memories to boost our morale when we need it, to bring a smile to our lips when we feel we just can't go on, then it will be possible to find ourselves happy most of the time. And isn't that what everybody wants?

To be happy is a choice. It is our choice. Nobody can make us happy but ourselves. Nobody can come and inject happiness into us. Happiness is found inside ourselves. It doesn't matter where you are—the type of house you own, the country you live in, the vehicle you drive, the job you have. It doesn't matter

---

[1] For this thought, I am indebted to Anthony Robbins, *Awaken the Giant Within* (New York: Simon & Schuster, 1992).

what you have—lots of jewelry, a good-looking spouse, great clothes, a pet or any other thing. You will always find yourself with—you guessed it—yourself![2] *What does this mean? It means that unless you learn to find happiness inside yourself, happiness will always be a myth, a desire, but not your reality.*

The devil will always try to convince us of his lies. He will try to fill our hearts with doubts and darkness. He will try his best to make us miss out on the best moments of our lives. But God wants us to be happy. He has made us with the capacity to be happy, and He wants to give us all the grace we need in order to be happy. So when we feel down or lonely, we can confidently call on Him and say: "Lord, I am kind of feeling blue today. Can You please help me to see all the blessings in my life? Please enfold me in Your love, and I shall sing with joy!"

---

[2] Anthony Robbins, *Awaken the Giant Within.*

Wisdom to contemplate:

"Rejoice in the Lord always. I shall say it again: rejoice!"
(Philippians 4:4)

"Happy the people so blessed; happy the people whose God is the LORD." (Psalm 144:15)

"I will delight and rejoice in you; I will sing hymns to your name, Most High." (Psalm 9:3)

The Birthday Party
–5–

Ellie was dressed in a dark blue sleeveless dress with white stripes; it was her favorite. Reuben used to travel a lot because of his new job, and every time he came home from a trip, he brought Ellie a new dress. Her collection was quite wonderful; nevertheless, this was the dress she had picked for this special day. She was bouncing around full of happiness, radiating joy because it was her birthday, the day on which everybody would make her feel special! She was ecstatic because finally she had found the piñata of her dreams—it was "Bert" from Sesame Street! This particular one was tough to find because it was hard to make, but Reuben had somehow managed to find it.

Yes, she loved her birthdays, and this particular one would be at a country club with endless green grass meadows and three huge pools. This meant that she and her friends would be able to run around, play games, eat cake and swim all in the same day. In her opinion, nothing could top that. All her friends were coming, and her mother had arranged all sorts of games and had outdone herself decorating the clubhouse.

Anna had also planned to have an illusionist come as a surprise, and so she needed a place where the kids could all sit together. Anna had arranged a multitude of colorful miniature chairs in a circle around the piñata. She surely knew how to throw a party! Illusionists had always been Ellie's favorite thing in the whole world, but she had never had the chance to see one up close and in person. She had always seen them on TV and marveled at the things they could do. Surely this would be an unforgettable day.

Everybody showed up, and everything turned out exactly as Anna had hoped; it was a great success. The piñata was loaded with what in Ellie's opinion was the most exquisite candy, and she had made Ellie a huge cake with Hansel and Gretel's candy house on top; it was a work of art. Ellie was so anxious to make her wishes and cut the cake, she couldn't wait until they sang "Happy birthday." She was already on the countdown to her three birthday wishes; after all, she had been carefully considering for months what to wish for.

Memories of her birthday parties were among Ellie's happiest. Lots of kids, lots of food, lots of balloons! Isn't that the recipe for a perfect day? Her mother would always make an enormous cake and have lots of little colorful surprises tied with colorful strings, full of trinkets and candy. Anna knew that you are a child only once. Therefore, she was determined to never underestimate what is important to a "little one." Since parties made Ellie so happy, when her birthday was near, Anna dedicated herself to planning the celebration with all her love. Ellie understood this, even at her young age; she not only understood it but appreciated it very much.

Ellie loved and cherished her mom. After all, she was her best friend. They were always having long talks. There was nothing they could not talk about—while Anna cooked, while they were doing errands, when Anna was taking a shower…anytime, all the time. Ellie simply adored her mother. She never got tired of hearing Anna's stories of when she and Ellie's grandmother were young. Even though Ellie was so small, her mother never treated her like a baby, and this created a special bond between them, a bond that would never be broken.

Ellie was now five years old.

A child's dream

Time spent together between a parent and a child is precious. The bond that is formed between mother and daughter or father and son in the early years is everlasting. By talking, a parent and a child learn to feel comfortable with each other, to open up and share.

A child can be therapeutic for a parent. Getting in touch with long forgotten memories stirs up emotions we have sometimes become unaware of. To see our children smile, to hear them laughing and to be there for the special moments in their lives is priceless.

Similarly, a parent can be the compass and the anchor in a child's life. A mom or dad can be a child's best friend without ever having to compromise discipline or authority. Being there for our children on a consistent, regular basis is very important, especially in their younger years when there are so many questions and so many fears. To share time together is healthy for both, and when the importance of spending time together is overlooked, this can become a parent's greatest regret.

Is there anything more important than for parents to spend time with their "little ones"? I find it hard to imagine. A mother, who spends time with her "little one" as Anna did with Ellie, will give her child self-confidence and a wisdom the child could hardly get anywhere else. Experiencing happy moments from the time we are small is very important. And no moments are more precious or happy to children than those spent with their parents. A parent who is there to listen is more valuable than any material thing parents could possibly buy for their children. Parents who are aware of and care about what their "little ones" think important will diminish the risk of disappointing them. Parents who are sensitive to their children's desires and dreams will be much more likely to make their children happy.

For a child, there are things that are of terrible importance, but a grown-up might not understand that unless the adult spends a lot of time with that child. The problem is not that the adult is indifferent to the child's feelings, but that the adult is simply not in tune with what is going on in the child's life. And parents might be so involved in their adult world that they have forgotten what was important when they were children themselves. It is just too easy for us to forget how important some things are when we are little. Children are very keen observers, and when children see that their parents are paying attention, they learn to rely on their parents for the rest of their lives.

It is true that many parents are working very hard trying to provide as much as they can for their children. This is admirable. But it would be a wonderful thing if every couple could try to have at least one parent at home, even if this means sacrificing some material comforts. There is nothing that is impossible for a heart that is determined. If we are determined to change our schedules, to change our lives, we will be able to do it.

True, in today's world, there are many single parents, and sometimes it is just not possible for a parent to be home. All we can do is do the best we can. But many parents do have a choice. Many could change things, but don't. Maybe in their minds they want to provide more for their children. But think about this: There is nothing more valuable or more important to give your children than to give them the gift of YOU!

Wisdom to contemplate:

*"With your whole heart honor your father;
your mother's birth pangs forget not.
Remember, of these parents you were born;
what can you give them for all they gave you?"
(Sirach 7:27)*

"Let your father and mother have joy; let her who bore you exult."(Proverbs 23:25)

So Fortunate

–6–

Reuben's new job demanded that he be ready to move to a different office every so many years. One day, Reuben was reassigned to an office abroad, and they had to move. Ellie did not quite understand what that meant, but her mother explained she would not see her friends again. She was not sure where the country was that they were going to, but her mother said it was very far from their current home. For the next few weeks, Ellie pondered whether she liked the idea or not. "Whatever happens though…I'll surely miss my friends," she thought to herself.

When the time came to leave, her kindergarten friend brought a teddy bear to the airport and quickly kissed her on the cheek to say goodbye.

For the first time in her short life, Ellie felt a bottomless sadness, a feeling she could not do anything about. She surrendered to it and hoped that it would eventually go away. She did not know that this was the beginning of how her whole life would be. This was the beginning of a new life. Her life as she knew it was now over. Like the Israelites, Ellie and her family experienced their own type of exodus. From now on, their life would be the life of nomads, a life of eternal change.

Ellie got lost in her thoughts. She wondered if she would have to do this for the rest of her life. She finally decided to share her worries with Anna. She knew Anna would have an answer, an explanation that would make her feel better.

"Mom I feel a little bit sad," Ellie said to Anna while she strongly gripped her stuffed animal.

"Do you think you can explain to me why? Is it because we are moving?" Anna asked her with tenderness.

"Mom, I just have so many things that worry me…I have so many questions in my head." Ellie told Anna her worries. She wondered if she would have to be on a never-ending journey—eternally finding a new house and trying to make it feel like home, only to have to move again later. Always dreading the first day of school, sure she would be stared at for being the "new one" in the class. Eternally meeting new people, trying hard to make friends and then, suddenly, without warning, leaving them again. Feeling ever so lonely for so long, finally making some friends and then finding herself at the airport, once again waving goodbye. Like a gypsy, forever coming and going, without a permanent place to call home.

Lovingly, Anna sat Ellie on her lap, and petted her cheek. "Ellie, you are a citizen of the world. Do you know what that means?"

Ellie shook her head "No".

"Being a citizen of the world means that instead of belonging to one place only, you belong to the whole world. Of course, as with everything else, this has its bright side as well as its difficult side. On one hand, you get to travel and see many different countries. You get to experience many different cultures with their languages, foods, dances and customs. Inevitably, you will become well rounded, and you will become a master at making friends, an expert at meeting new people, an authority on facing challenging new situations and succeeding in them. You will become outgoing and friendly, self-confident and self-reliant. You will become a connoisseur after becoming a conqueror. Do you understand what I am trying to say, Ellie?"

Ellie nodded and exhaled a sigh of relief. She felt so much better. "A citizen of the world," she repeated in her head until she slowly fell asleep in her mother's arms. A citizen of the world…that is what she would be.

What is life teaching us?

There are many trade-offs to the hardships that come with constant traveling and moving around. But, in the end we will find ourselves becoming very interesting people. We will have learned lessons that could not have been learned otherwise, lessons about other people and lessons about ourselves. Not everybody has the opportunity to partake of this type of life, so if we have had such an opportunity, we should be grateful to God for giving us such a gift. But we must always keep in mind that the joys of moving come as a package with the sorrows of departing.

There are many types of lives...from the life of sedentary people who were born and raised in the city in which they live to the life of nomads who have moved around all their lives. After considering the different types of life, I have only one thing to say: We should feel blessed whichever our life is like. Yes, we should feel blessed, because our lives are unique and precious. We live through the experiences, adventures and situations that have a potential of becoming great learning experiences. There is nothing impossible for God, and His specialty is to turn bad situations around and to make them a blessing in our lives. We are in this world to grow in holiness and to experience this wonderful world God has so lovingly created for us. And whatever comes our way, come what may, we experience exactly the situations we were meant to experience, exactly as we were meant to experience them. Everything in our lives has a purpose—to make us grow; to make our spirit, our mind and our heart grow; to help us grow in our knowledge and love of God and in our knowledge and love of our neighbor.

So, no matter what our life is like, no matter what the situation, we must never fail to search for what it is that God is teaching us. Let's take the time and ask ourselves:

- *What can I learn from this?*
- *Where is it taking me?*
- *What lessons am I supposed to be learning?*
- *What can I change?*
- *How can I be better?*

These are all important questions because they remind us that nothing happens by accident, everything happens for a reason and everything is perfect.

When we ask ourselves a question, it is important that we look for an answer. Jesus said, "Seek and you will find" (Matthew 7:7). If we ask, our minds will find answers that will help us understand the various situations and different moments of our lives. Even when a particular situation might be dragging us down and we barely have the strength to carry on, if we manage to hold on and ask the right questions, we will soon see wonderful changes—changes in the way we feel, changes in the way we think and changes in the way things seem.[3] *We will see clearly that things can change in a moment and that there is much to be learned. Even in the toughest times, we can find the right answers, and the right approach. We are blessed to have the chance to live through situations that will give us wisdom and that will mold our character. We are exactly where we are meant to be.*

The Bible tells us we are citizens of heaven. What a wonderful citizenship to have! We belong to heaven, and this beautiful world was made for us. How special are we? How great is God's love for us? That thought is enough to enable us to feel special no matter how our lives have been. It is marvelous to know God made this wonderful world just for us. Understanding that we are citizens of heaven should be enough to bring a smile to our faces every day of our lives!

---

[3] Anthony Robbins, *Awaken the Giant Within.*

Wisdom to contemplate:

"But our citizenship is in heaven, and from it we also await a savior, the Lord Jesus Christ."
(Philippians 3:20)

"The earth is the LORD'S and all it holds, the world and those who live there. For God founded it on the seas, established it over the rivers. (Psalm 24:1)

Beyond Frontiers

–7–

The new country was beautiful, like nothing Ellie had ever imagined. It was extraordinary. When she exited the airplane, she felt a bit chilly; it was like the wind was taking little bites off her cheeks.

From the balcony of her new house, Ellie could see what to her was an endless mountain covered with snow. It seemed as if it was completely vertical, and it was simply magnificent. She daydreamed about how extraordinary it would be if one day she went on an expedition to climb it to the top. She was not afraid of the dangerous heights—she was fascinated by the thought of being so close to God.

In the beginning, the new country was just great. After all, it was a dazzling place full of things to see and do. Ellie traveled a lot around the country and had the opportunity to try delicious foods she had never tasted before. She had the opportunity to see many animals she had never seen before: giant turtles, llamas and condors. She saw indigenous peoples who lived in the rain forest; they carried long shafts, painted their bodies and colored their hair red. Other native people lived in the city; the women wore lots of necklaces around their throats and carried their babies on their backs. The men played instruments she had never heard before; the instruments seemed to be telling sad songs about the past. For the most part, both men and women had long braided hair. Usually the men dressed in white with black hats, and the women in long black skirts with colorful blouses and black shawls.

Anna said, "Ellie, we are so blessed! Because not many people have the opportunity we are having. You know, Ellie, many people live their lives wishing they could travel, but they do not get the chance. So now you have a responsibility to learn and enjoy as much as possible since you have been given this chance. Then, later in life, you will be able to share your experiences, telling them firsthand to a friend or someone from work. Or maybe you will write a book. Drill all these images and experiences into your head. Paint a beautiful picture that you may share one day, so people can see through your eyes the beauty of the countries you have visited. OK?"

"OK, Mom," Ellie said, while she frantically looked around trying not to miss a thing, hypnotized by all the novelties.

Ellie was determined to make a mental picture of everything she was seeing—a mental picture that she would never erase as long as she lived! It was the first time she saw with her own two eyes that there are in fact many types of people in the world and that there is a lot of beauty that comes with meeting them. It was one thing to be told that such things existed, but another thing to actually experience them.

Anna was very happy because she knew this was a golden opportunity for her and her family. "The world indeed is a beautiful place, Ellie. It is full of lovely people to meet and places to discover. Just when you think that you have seen the most amazing place in the world, God winks at you and startles you by giving you the opportunity to see a more beautiful place…one more magical creation overflowing with His love!"

They were looking out from their balcony, cuddled up together under a big shawl. They each had a steaming hot cup of cocoa in their hands and were simply happy to be alive. Ellie was in awe, recognizing how extraordinary it all was. No movie, no fairy tale, no book could compare to the real world!

Ellie was six years old.

Expanding our horizons

Even if we do not get a chance to live abroad, it is important that we make an effort to learn about other countries and cultures. The more well rounded we are, the more understanding we will be with people who might seem different to us. When we make an effort to learn a different language and use it with a native speaker of that language, then we will realize how hard it is for others to communicate with us, and we will become more appreciative of their efforts. Even if we only learn a little bit and even if we feel like a fool when we are trying to speak, people will appreciate our efforts. We must not be afraid to learn other languages; it will open many frontiers for us. It will break the ice between us and the people from that special country we visit. We will win over their hearts. I guarantee you they will be more candid with us and more willing to help.

When we make an effort to look beyond our frontiers and really pay attention, we become more sensitive to the rest of the world. And we become more aware that we are not just what we know; we are part of a much greater thing. This allows us to become more compassionate and more involved with the world in general. It allows us to become more sensitive and more grateful. It allows us to understand that we are part of a greater plan. As a result, we will experience interior growth, and our minds will expand. We will be fairer in our opinions about a certain country or about a foreigner who is struggling to succeed and survive in our country. We might also decide to become missionaries and go to serve the Lord in a faraway land. Missionaries serve God while learning firsthand what a beautiful world God has made.

The fact that we don't see something doesn't mean it doesn't exist; it also doesn't mean that it is not important and cannot be significant to us. It is up to us to take an interest and to learn about what is out there for us. It is our choice to open our minds and hearts, not only to the beauty of our country or our continent but to the beauty of the whole world God has created for us.

Wisdom to contemplate:

" It happens that there are many different languages in the world, and none is meaningless; but if I do not know the meaning of a language, I shall be a foreigner to one who speaks it, and one who speaks it a foreigner to me."
(1 Corinthians 14:10-11)

"He said to them, 'Go into the whole world and proclaim the gospel to every creature.'" (Mark 16:15)

"For God so loved the world that he gave his only Son, so that everyone who believes in him might not perish but might have eternal life." (John 3:16)

The Bedtime Prayer
–8–

Every night before going to sleep, Reuben would come into Ellie's room to pray. He explained to Ellie that God loves us all but that He especially loves "little ones." For example, Jesus had made a point of telling everyone just how special "little ones" were to Him. For this reason, she should always pray at the end of the day, giving thanks for all the good things she had, asking God for the things that were important to her and telling Him just how great she thought He was.

Before reciting her individual prayers, he taught her to say a simple prayer that Ellie loved:

"Little child Jesus…I want to be better than yesterday. I want to be like you …little child Jesus."

Every night, without exception, she said this prayer. She said it with a fervor that made her father wonder how a child her age could be so full of faith.

After this prayer, she used to review her day and made sure she did not forget any of the things she was grateful for. She felt so close to Jesus. She could not explain it, but somehow she was sure He was right there next to her every day of her life. She never doubted this fact; she never questioned His existence, not because she was naive or ingenuous but because an absolute certainty dwelled deep inside her heart. She knew He was a reality because she could feel Him.

Reuben knew there was a special relationship between Ellie and Jesus. He was sure her guardian angels were always buzzing around. If not, how then could you explain that special shine she had? She was so full of faith at that age that the only possible explanation was that she was able to experience Jesus' love in a very real way. Somehow Reuben knew Ellie was one of Jesus' "special little ones."

The importance of our religion

Talking about Christianity lately has become almost taboo. Many parents would rather have their children believe in nothing than give them guidance and teach them about religion. It may be because they do not have faith themselves, or simply because they are full of doubts. Sometimes maybe they would rather "wash their hands" of the whole matter than have their kids complain to them later in life about the faith they were taught.

So, children grow up with no spiritual guidance. All they hear in school and the media is: "All religions are right." "We need to be inclusive." "We cannot offend others by sharing our beliefs!" And so on.

But this is not the right approach because it suggests there is no need for us to pick one! Some people think all religions are right, but they should at least realize that all the religions do not have the fullness of the truth. The fact that some believe all religions are right does not mean that we should stay lukewarm and not go deeply into our Christian faith. We need to be on fire, full of love for God. If we are not, in the long run we will have a void and feel a deep emptiness within us.

Someone once said, "If we don't teach them, someone else will." When children and adolescents grow up with no spiritual guidance, it is almost guaranteed that they will lose their path. We must teach what is pleasing to God. We need to be the light of the world, just as Jesus asked us to be. We need to teach obedience and self-control; after all, Christ calls us to obedience. Just as there are laws that rule the universe and the world, so there are laws that rule us—laws for which we are accountable to our God and to our neighbor. The Bible reminds us: "So then each of us shall give an account of himself to God." (Romans 14:12)

Why do you think there are so many problems today with children and teenagers? Why do you think there are problems such as school shootings, gang violence and teenage pregnancy? Why should we be surprised at how easy it is for children to pull a trigger if we have never taught them that there are just some things in life that are absolutely wrong? What stops a child who has never been taught the way to live a good life? What stops a child who has not learned any boundaries and is not afraid of anything? What stops a child who has never been taught that there are consequences to all our actions? Christianity is our only hope because it teaches the truth. We cannot underestimate the danger of not teaching what is right and what is wrong and, most important, what pleases God.

We must not be indifferent to our Christian religion. Our religion contains the story of our salvation. Our religion is us acting on God's gift to us.

Our religion is our compass to Christ, and Christ is our way to heaven. Through our religion, we learn about God's love; we learn to trust Him and respect Him. We open our hearts to Him when we learn how Jesus Christ came to this world and died for our sins on the cross. We understand that He rose from the dead, and so today we can truly rejoice and sing a song that says, "I am saved. I have been rescued by the arms of Jesus." Thinking about God's gift of everlasting life to us transforms our lives. Knowing that He loved us first and not because we deserved it or because of any merit of ours but simply because He is love itself and we are precious to Him—this makes all the difference. This amazing truth is enough to make us people of joy, people of love, people of truth, people of obedience, people who belong to Christ. So vital a truth should not be hidden, suppressed or kept for later. We must investigate it, study it, share it and make it part of our life.

So many people become complacent, living a life that is empty. They feel this emptiness, so they try to fill it with many things, only to find out that they still feel this void inside. Until we soothe our spirit with God's goodness, until we fulfill our spiritual need by finding God's saving love, we will not be able to find true happiness.

Many people go to a psychologist, putting all their faith in the services of a professional caregiver. And the psychologist does his or her best, trying to find a psychological cause for the problem. The doctor finds a logical reason and prescribes a medicine. But if the soul is not healed, the medicine will give only temporary relief, a temporary fix. We must go to the root of the problem. If we want to permanently find happiness, joy and peace, we must first be embraced by God's healing love!

Wisdom to contemplate:

"'*Everything is lawful for me,' but not everything is beneficial. 'Everything is lawful for me,' but I will not let myself be dominated by anything*." *(1 Corinthians 6:12).*

"But you, man of God, avoid all this. Instead, pursue righteousness, devotion, faith, love, patience, and gentleness. Compete well for the faith. Lay hold of eternal life, to which you were called when you made the noble confession in the presence of many witnesses. (1 Timothy 6:11-12)

"Amen, amen, I say to you, whoever believes has eternal life." (John 6:47)

"Tell them to do good, to be rich in good works, to be generous, ready to share, thus accumulating as treasure a good foundation for the future, so as to win the life that is true life." (1 Timothy 6:18-19)

Cruel Kids

–9–

At the beginning, things were OK at Ellie's new school. But as she got a little older and she had to go to first grade, things became more difficult. It was hard to make friends in elementary school. The children had changed, and the new ones seemed to be an impenetrable bunch. Nobody was being nice to her. They were calling her names and playing tricks on her.

"Giant Potato, you are too big to be in our class!" yelled one.

"Your freckles make you look like a banana…banana!" shouted another.

"Why don't you try to get a tan…cup of milk!" loudly said yet another.

All this name calling was hard for Ellie. "Why are they being mean to me? Don't they know they are hurting my feelings?" she wondered. The fact of the matter was that she had done nothing to them except exist. Maybe she was too happy for their liking. She was not good at defending herself, maybe because all she could feel was sadness. Her mind would freeze, and she would just stand there like a little puppy that has been frightened and humiliated by human yelling.

Ellie had always been a big girl for her age. Even compared to the boys, she was very tall. When the teacher formed the children into a line to go somewhere out of the classroom, Ellie was always the last one. Her other big problem was that she had very light skin. She was not an albino, but, compared to most of the kids in her class, who had darker or tanned skin, she seemed pretty white. She had a few freckles, like cinnamon sprinkled over fresh apples. The freckles gave her character and adorned her charming girly face. But to top it all off, when she tried to defend herself by telling them that she was a princess, they told her that she was not and that she was a dummy for believing that. "Yes I am…I am," she repeated. But all they did was laugh.

She was aware of her big feet, but, as her mom had said, how else would she be able to stand? After all, she was a tall girl. If she had tiny little feet, she would just fall on her face.

"You have always been beautiful. You know that in many places being tall is considered a great quality. Models need to be tall. There are no short models on the catwalks in Paris, for example! And Princess Grace was fair-skinned just like you, Ellie," Anna said. And as for being fat—Anna told Ellie it was just a bit of baby fat that would go away with time—"nothing a little exercising cannot remedy if you need it when you are older."

Ellie also thought about how Anna had said freckles made people interesting. And that the reason she was white was that she had European ancestors and in many European countries people have very light skin.

The curious thing was that these were all things Ellie found out about herself in her new school. Before going to elementary school, she had not been aware of her looks. She had had no idea if she was fat or skinny, tall or short, dark or light. To herself, she was just a normal little girl—other than the fact, of course, that she was a princess!

When Ellie would come home crying and tell her mom what had happened in school, Anna would remain very calm. Lovingly caressing Ellie's head, she would explain:

"Look, Ellie, there will always be people who will try to make fun of you, even as you get older. Some people do this to feel better about themselves because if they can prove to themselves that others are ugly, then they can be confident they look better. Other people are just jealous and insecure, so they get full of envy. Envy is terrible. It is like a disease that quickly takes you over and makes you a bitter, mean person. It can make you someone who's never able to rejoice with other people's good fortune. Don't ever be jealous of anyone, Ellie. Be happy about other people's blessings, and be confident that you, too, have been blessed. Maybe you have not been blessed in the same areas as they have, but if you pay attention to your life instead of other people's lives, then you will soon see how blessed you are indeed.

"Some people are just trying to be funny at someone else's expense, they do it to get attention, and they end up hurting other people's feelings. Yet others are just ignorant; since they have never seen anyone different before, they assume everybody should look like them. Ignorance is simply lack of knowledge. When people don't know something, they are more likely to hate it or not like it, maybe because it scares them, maybe because it makes them feel insecure. In any event, now that you have traveled a bit, you understand that everybody in the world is different. So there is no reason to feel sad just because you don't look exactly like the majority does. It just means you are unique, special.

"Look, Ellie, we cannot live our lives trying to please others because we will never be able to do that. There will always be someone for whom we are too fat, too thin, too white, too dark, too tall, too short. We have to be happy with who we know we are and know that even if in other people's opinion we are not so beautiful, our personalities can still win their hearts. Looks don't matter as long as you have a great personality and are always kind and full of love instead of being angry with others. Then, Ellie, you will shine, and no matter what others think about the way you look, they will be charmed by your self-confidence, good humor and wittiness. If they still don't like you, it just means they are not worth being around—just keep your distance, and try to ignore them

"So leave beauty to luck. Maybe in people's opinion you will be a beautiful girl. Maybe you won't. But as long as you don't care, then there is no problem. Put your efforts into what you can control, into your personality and your heart. These things you can always improve, always change. These are the things that will make you special and that will make you an extraordinary person, a princess!

'The most important thing that you should learn from this experience is to always know in your heart that beauty is relative. It depends on opinions. Just make sure that in your opinion you are the most beautiful girl in the world—and you should know that for us you are! This is called being confident, and this is very important, so that others can't hurt you.

"Don't ever say something mean to anybody, especially if you think it is true, because you will hurt their feelings. And once you speak something, you can never take back your words. Don't ever be mean. Always be shining with happiness and love, never show bitterness and anger, and you will always be our princess. You might not be the princess to a whole kingdom, but you are our princess. Just ignore them; after all, you know in your heart what you are. Whatever they say you are is just their opinion, nothing more, nothing less. It does not mean they are right. Why give them so much importance?"

Ellie did not know that by experiencing these things she was learning the biggest lesson of her life.

Ellie never forgot the things her mother told her because her mother's words were soothing to her heart. They had a calming effect on her, like sinking her body into warm, calm water. She felt blessed and cherished because of how loving her parents were. As usual, Anna had given her an answer that she could understand and that made her feel good about herself, an answer that would be valuable to her throughout her whole life. It didn't stop the kids from making fun of her, but it sure stopped her from feeling sad and losing her self-confidence.

Ellie was seven years old.

The importance of self-confidence

Isn't it ironic, that it is only after growing up a bit that we start becoming aware of our looks? I don't think many parents realize the importance of teaching their children to be kind. And I don't think many parents realize how much a child can suffer in school. In some people's opinion, children don't have problems, only adults. But this is not true. Everything is proportional to the person experiencing it. For little children, a problem that can seem trivial to an adult can deeply hurt their feelings and leave them heartbroken.

Kids can be cruel sometimes, bruising their peers in the most profound way, shattering their self-confidence, making them feel miserable, utterly disappointed and troubled. Fortunately, some "little ones" have been blessed with wise and loving parents. A mother or a father who always has the right words to say is the best antidote for a child's distress. Words have the power to heal us and to change our day no matter what age we are. But even if someone has not been blessed with good human parents, God is always there, and He always manages to bring His comforting love to us when we need it.

But if a person does not know God and does not have good guidance from their parents, then they run the risk of becoming mean or of developing huge complexes that later in life will be very hard to overcome. Sometimes when people are trying to hurt us, it is because they are hurting very badly inside themselves. Or they may have a fear of rejection—so, before we have a chance to reject them, they reject us. People have lives we don't understand and don't know. We must try hard to never be mean back, always assuming they are sad and lonely people. Therefore, we should feel compassion for them, understanding they probably are unhappy at home.

Not everybody is nice in the world, but that that does not mean everybody is mean. Not everybody is nice in the world, but that is no reason to join them. There will always be mean people, jealous people, angry people, bitter people and envious people in our lives. But there will always be good, kind, friendly, compassionate, caring people, too. So, we must open our eyes and search for the people who are worth our while, instead of getting disappointed thinking that people are all bad. By giving a chance to others, we are really giving a chance to ourselves.

It is of the utmost importance to make sure we do not become infected by bitterness or become mean ourselves. We must make an effort to always be excellent, no matter how hard things get. When someone says something to us, we have to know it is not a fact, but just a disputable opinion that person has about us. We should not let it bother us. An opinion is just a guess, a supposition, a generalization somebody makes about us. It is harmless unless we allow it to become important, since it will not be true unless we make it true. Why give people or words an importance that they do not deserve?

We all have encountered at some point in time someone trying to hurt us. Let's be more confident inside from now on, remembering that anything anybody says about us is just their opinion. Why do we insist on being offended by what other people say? Who cares what someone else calls me if I know who I am for real? Why should it be such a tragedy to be called a name? Who cares? Why do we insist on giving so much importance to other people's opinions of us? We need to know, understand and appreciate our qualities so that no mean comment about us can tear us apart. People's words only are as powerful as we give them the power to be. A harsh word will have no intensity, and a mean comment will mean nothing if we do not give them any meaning. They will have no effect if we do not give them importance. A mean word will be a wasted effort as long as we do not allow it to bother us.

We cannot change certain people, but we can ignore them. We cannot change certain people, but we can always change ourselves. Let's therefore focus on ourselves that we may be stronger and turn into better people, so that we can keep a good equilibrium in this world bringing to it goodness and love. Let's make a point out of becoming more confident. To be sure of ourselves is one of the most valuable lessons we will ever learn, and it is never too late. Let's make it our goal to find reasons to be happy instead of reasons to be offended. Let's make it our life's task to learn to be less mean. After all, after a while the mean people may get tired of being mean, and after a while being nice and kind becomes contagious.

Wisdom to contemplate:

"Rejoice in hope, endure in affliction, persevere in prayer." (Romans 12:12)

Continue your kindness toward your friends, your just defense of the honest heart. Do not let the foot of the proud overtake me, nor the hand of the wicked disturb me." (Psalm 36:11-12)

"Trust in the LORD and do good that you may dwell in the land and live secure. Find your delight in the LORD who will give you your heart's desire. Commit your way to the LORD; trust that God will act and make your integrity shine like the dawn, your vindication like noonday. Be still before the LORD; wait for God. Do not be provoked by the prosperous, nor by malicious schemers. Give up your anger, abandon your wrath; do not be provoked; it brings only harm." (Psalm 37:3)

Esoteric Experience
–10–

There had been a suicide in the house Ellie and her family now lived in, and Lala their maid was aware of this. One of the rooms in the basement was always kept locked, because the dead man's family had left his belongings there. Ellie and her brother Johnny used to peek into the room from the garden through a small window set close to the ground. They always thought it was spooky because most of the furniture was covered with white bed sheets that were full of dust and spider webs. Johnny loved to frighten Ellie by telling her he was sure the house was haunted. But Anna always convinced Ellie that Johnny had nothing better to do, so he was just trying to have some fun at her expense by making up stories.

One night, Ellie's parents had gone out to a dinner party, and her siblings had gone out to other parties, leaving her home alone with the maid.

Lala was a mysterious indigenous woman. She was short and tubby with very long black braids framing the deep wrinkles in her face. These wrinkles told the story of a laborious and arduous life, because, before coming to the city, Lala had lived in the mountains, and life in the mountains is never easy.

Lala was always dressed in the traditional indigenous dress: a long black wool skirt, a colorful blouse with lots of embroidery and a black shawl. Lala frequently told enigmatic stories about her people, about the past and about some things Ellie didn't quite understand, mostly Indian legends and beliefs. For example, she told Ellie about the "Day of the Dead" that is celebrated in that country by both indigenous and white people. Every year, the people prepare a special drink that has a pungent taste and is deep purple in color. They also prepare a special bread, sometimes meticulously arranged in the shape of a dead person, to bring to the cemetery and offer to the dead. They visit the cemeteries at night to leave the offerings and sing sad songs about days long gone.

"Not all of the living go to heaven or hell after they die," Lala said in a mystic tone. "For whatever reason, some souls seem to get stuck between the two planes, and they return from the dead to disturb us and spook us."

"But why, Lala? Why would they come to bother us?" Ellie asked in a puzzled, squeaky voice.

"Because some of them are bored. Some just want to communicate with us and befriend us, yet others are just angry at the fact that they are still around," Lala stated in a very convincing, almost hypnotic way.

Ellie's eyes opened wide and became huge, reflecting her fear, reflecting scenes of ghosts hunting her. She was easily frightened, and Lala's stories had frightened her badly. "You have a gift, Ellie," Lala continued "and for this reason it will always be easier for you to see them or hear them. They will try to communicate with you. This is why you must learn to control your fear and dominate your gift. Fear will never help you in a bad situation. Fear must be conquered. Do you understand?"

Ellie nodded, but she could feel her legs growing weaker, and she could feel a teardrop starting to make its way down her cheek.

Lala was not trying to scare Ellie. In her mind, she was helping the little girl. In fact, Ellie did have a gift. Some call it ESP, others psychic abilities. The name is not important. In any event, Ellie was very sensitive. As far as Lala was concerned, the problem is that when a person has this sensitivity, the doors to other realms open, but they open for both positive and negative entities. There is no way of controlling if the entity that will contact us will bring a good energy or a bad one. The doors open to all that is out there. Therefore, the old woman saw it as her duty to teach Ellie about controlling both the gift and her fears.

On this night, though, Lala would confirm Ellie's biggest fear. "Indeed, the house is inhabited by the spirit of the man who committed suicide in it," Lala said coldly. Ellie could not believe her ears when Lala told her this. To make matters worse, the electricity went out right after Lala had told her this. Was it a coincidence? Maybe…and then again maybe not.

"Ellie, do not worry," Lala said. "I will light a candle, and everything will be OK. Darkness always gives in to light…don't forget this. This is one of the most valuable things you will ever learn." As she said this, she had already found a long white candle and was lighting it. "Today is the perfect day for us to be alone in this house while it is dark, because I want you to experience the gift you have."

They stood at the base of the stairs that went up to the second floor. Lala asked Ellie if she could see the glow coming from her parents' room. Indeed, Ellie could see a bright glow coming from exactly that direction.

But just when Lala was about to make Ellie go toward the glow on her own, Ellie's parents came home. Ellie felt relieved and happy to see them. She felt as if she had been about to fall into an abyss and someone had saved her by grabbing her by the shirt collar.

Anna had had a feeling they should head home earlier than planned, and Reuben had driven them home in a heartbeat. Anna was glad that as usual she had trusted her instincts. She was upset that Lala had taken things so far. After all, Ellie was still only a little girl, and Lala's stories and beliefs were too scary for Ellie to handle. Anna was very happy that she had come on time. Ellie quickly forgot about the incident, at least until she had her next experience a few years later. Ellie was now eight years old.

The dangers of fear

Fear is normal and natural. Many times, our fears are even well founded. So it is not good to deny our fears or to try to suppress them. Our fears should be confronted and beaten. Sometimes what we need to do to defeat a fear is to share it with someone—a loved one, an advisor, a teacher, a friend. Other times, we can do research and read about the subject and see how others feel about it. Many times, sharing with others and realizing that others go through the same fears help us deal with our own fears.

Fear is something we all have to deal with at some point or another. It can be fear about events in our daily life, such as losing our job, getting sick, getting into an accident or losing our loved ones. Or it can be fear about more intangible things, such as fear of certain unexplained experiences. When we were younger, many of us have suffered from fear after watching scary movies about Dracula, Freddy Krueger or poltergeists. Many of us have spent nights without sleep. Many of us have had horrible nightmares or strange dreams, and some of us might even have had weird, unexplainable experiences while we were awake.

Fear can be our worse enemy. The best way to beat our fears is to call on God's help. He is the Almighty, and under His wings we can take refuge. All we have to do is pray and call on the power of His name, and He will deliver us from our fears before we know it.

But still, as always, we must do our part. One successful way to protect ourselves from our fears is not to obsess about them. There are many unexplained things here on this earth. We do not need to look into all of them. If we knock, the door will be opened...but we must be careful where we are knocking. Let's be careful about what we mess with. Some things can easily get out of our control. Let's set boundaries for ourselves, so that we do not accidentally fall victim to what we are most afraid of. We should stay away from the dark side of life, in other words we should stay away from the occult. If we choose to stay in the light, we will minimize our chances of getting hurt physically or psychologically. Let's not mess with the esoteric. Let's let some mysteries remain mysteries. And let's put our focus and our trust on God. Our Father in heaven loves us and wants to keep us safe under His umbrella of protection.

We must trust our instincts. Every time we get a bad feeling about something we cannot explain, we should try to listen to it. There are many reasons why we might get a feeling about a particular thing. Not everything can be explained logically, but this does not mean that it is not real. If we become people who rely only on facts, then we will limit ourselves to the five senses, and that will not give us a complete picture. Quantum physics has demonstrated that nothing has been proven for sure and that everything is possible. Time after time, something scientists believed to be the absolute truth has been proven wrong. Now scientists know only one thing is for sure, and that is that nothing is for sure.[4] *We cannot choose to ignore the fact that life is a mystery, and therefore we must always leave room for the benefit of the doubt—even for those things we don't want to believe in.*

Fear is something to be respected but not something to be intimidated by. Fear is something to be watchful for, but not something to obsess about. Feeling afraid can sometimes be a warning signal, to advise us not to go in a certain direction or to act in a certain manner. Our fears can be our best friends because they can warn us about areas in our lives we need to be careful about. Other times, fears are the products of our imaginations, and they must be controlled.

One thing is essential—and that is to not let ourselves be conquered or frozen by our fears. We need to have faith and trust that God always takes care of us. God is more powerful than anything, and He loves us and protects us. When we are afraid, we need to think about how God is our refugee and our fortress, and repeat that to ourselves. We who are sheltered under His shadow and are protected by His loving wings must cling to Him in our darkest

---

[4] Gary Zukav, *The Dancing Wu Li Masters* (Harper Collins, 2001).

moments. If we call upon Him, He will protect us. There need be no doubt in our hearts.

Wisdom to contemplate:

"Have no anxiety at all, but in everything, by prayer and petition, with thanksgiving, make your requests known to God. Then the peace of God that surpasses all understanding will guard your hearts and minds in Christ Jesus." (Philippians 4:6-7)

"You who dwell in the shelter of the Most High, who abide in the shadow of the Almighty, say to the LORD, 'My refuge and fortress, my God in whom I trust.' God will rescue you from the fowler's snare, from the destroying plague, will shelter you with pinions, spread wings that you may take refuge; God's faithfulness is a protecting shield. You shall not fear the terror of the night nor the arrow that flies by day, nor the pestilence that roams in darkness, nor the plague that ravages at noon.

The Big Surprise

–11–

Everything from the whole house was now packed inside a container, heading toward their new destination. Yes, Ellie's family had been transferred one more time.

In their new location, Ellie's family quickly found a house they liked. It was a big white house that Ellie fell in love with the first moment she saw it. For the first time, she had her own room, and she was eager to decorate it to her own taste.

One day, Anna and Ellie were driving around the neighborhood in order to get aquatinted with their surroundings. Suddenly, Ellie saw a big sign that read "Cuddly Puppies for Sale!" Ellie begged Anna to stop the car so they could take a look at the puppies. That was Anna's big mistake. Everybody knows that "seeing puppies" means "buying a puppy". Anna bought Ellie a black, curly, cuddly, male cockapoo—a mix between a cocker spaniel and a poodle. Ellie named him "Jelly Bean," and she made sure he was always by her side.

She had recently registered at her new school, and, as usual, she was nervous about the first day. She bought all her school supplies and her uniform and anxiously waited for Monday to come. She barely lived through Sunday, and that was only because she had Jelly Bean to distract her. Otherwise, she would have died from waiting with such apprehension.

As she had anticipated, she was once again the tallest student in the class. In the beginning, the other children were curious, trying to find out who this new girl was. It was a break from the monotony of the school to have someone new. Some were pretty friendly. Others kept a distance. In general, she thought it had been a pretty successful day.

A long year passed since that first day of school. Ellie was happy because until now she had had a very quiet school year. She was sitting in the back of the bus, next to a thin, blonde girl, who was oblivious to her because she was hypnotized by the music in her iPod. When Ellie arrived at school, there was an unusual buzzing. She did not know why, but all the kids looked very excited.

"Did you hear? Menudo is coming, and Manuela Valencia is going to be the one taking them around the city?!" one of the kids said to her. It turned out that Manuela Valencia was the daughter of the owner of the biggest chain of TV and radio stations in the country. Manuela was going to be handpicking a group of girls to be her "Menudo fan club," of which she would be the president.

Ellie adored the group Menudo, especially Charlie, one of the handsome 15-year-old singers. She had all their records and posters. She had never gone to one of their concerts, but she had seen all their movies and knew most of their songs by heart. Elli was dying to go to the concert, and she was confident this should not be hard to orchestrate. Anna would take her. She would give anything for a chance to meet them, but she had a slim-to-none chance to be part of this momentous occasion. Manuela not only was not Ellie's friend, but she had never really shown any interest in her. Manuela was just too popular. Everybody wanted to be her friend, and she had too many people around her all the time. But this kind of opportunity would never present itself again, and Ellie knew it! She could not miss this chance; this was the opportunity of a lifetime. But what could she do to get Manuela's attention and get her to like her enough to make her part of the event? She could never have imagined how things would develop and how the matter would turn out.

One day at the library, out of the blue, Manuela turned to Ellie and said, "Hi, Ellie. I have always wanted to be your friend but never really had the chance to meet you. How would you like to be part of the Menudo fan club?" Manuela stood in front of Ellie, smiling with bouncy enthusiasm, then continued, "I think this would give us a good chance to get to know each other!"

Ellie felt numb, and her mouth was open. She just could not help it. This was weird to say the least. Was she dreaming? Had she fallen asleep at the library? Was she having an unusually vivid dream?

She was not dreaming. Manuela had, in fact, asked her to be part of her fan club. But a few days later, without warning, Manuela's parents put a limit on how many kids could come to the house at any given time, and apologetically Manuela had to cut Ellie from the club. Ellie felt as if someone had dropped a huge piano onto her. She had been so excited. Her dream had "almost" come true. But almost doesn't count, now does it? What was worse was that she had got all excited—and for what? "For nothing," she thought to herself miserably.

That day, Ellie came straight home from school, went immediately into her bedroom and lay down. Anna knew something was wrong because Ellie would always come home from school, change clothes and go play with Jelly Bean.

When Anna found out about Ellie's disappointment, she felt very sorry for her, particularly because she knew how much this had meant to her. Ellie tried hard not to make a big deal out of what had happened and managed to keep a good attitude. She tried hard to distract herself, and in the meantime she put away all her Menudo posters and records.

Behind the scenes, Anna kept thinking of ways to make Ellie's dream come true. She had a good friend in an all-girls school in which, on the Saturday before the big concert, there would be a special private concert. Secretly, Anna managed to obtain two tickets. Her friend also promised to help them get in early, so that Ellie might have a chance to meet the group, before or after they had their meeting with the press.

Anna wanted to surprise Ellie. She came into Ellie's room and gave her a colorful envelope. The envelope read:

"Small miracles always happen to faithful people."

Ellie opened it, and there they were—two tickets to Menudo's special concert. She could not believe her eyes. After all, this concert was only for a select few; not even the girls from the fan club were allowed to come. How had this happened? How had her mom managed this? How did Ellie get so lucky? Millions of questions rushed through her head. The only other concert Menudo would have was on the next day, and it had been sold out a long time before Ellie even knew they were coming. She had lost all hope of even seeing them in concert. She was baffled at how things had unfolded. "Thank you, Jesus," she silently prayed, "because you understand that sometimes little things can mean a lot for a little girl like me!"

On the day of the concert, Ellie was running around her room like a headless chicken. She kept trying on clothes and changing her mind. The room was a complete mess—pants, skirts and blouses everywhere. She didn't have a lot of time to spare. She finally made up her mind and got ready. She looked gorgeous; she had on a plain pair of jeans and a short blue T-shirt that allowed her belly button to show slightly.

Ellie was a tall girl, and she looked older than her age. She was as tall as Anna now, and her brown hair had gotten long and curly enough to be wild while still looking soft and innocent. Her eyes were still as blue as the sky, and they seemed to possess a special shine. When she looked at someone, that person could not help but notice how beautiful her eyes were. But what was most special about her was not that she had turned into a gorgeous young woman, but that, as usual, she was shining!

That day was unforgettable. Not only were Anna and Ellie able to get there early, but they sneaked in right before the security guards stopped allowing people into the press room. By chance, Ellie spotted a group member who was not being harassed by anyone. The reason was that he was a new member, substituting for one of the other kids who had gotten too old to be part of the group. She was initially a bit disappointed because it was impossible to get close to the other members. She was not so interested in going to a new member she knew nothing about and asking him for an autograph. After all, he was not in any of her posters and of course not in any of the movies she had seen. He was just too new. To her, he was just another kid, and other than the fact that he was dressed in the Menudo outfit, nothing gave away the fact that he was a member of the famous group.

Anna understood that he was probably feeling awkward. "Ellie, put yourself in his shoes. How would you feel if all the girls and the press were going after the other members and almost no one was paying attention to you?" Anna said. "Go up to him and introduce yourself. Ask for an autograph, and be kind, because he is most definitively very nervous and more than a bit disappointed."

Ellie felt a bit awkward but approached him anyway. She said, "Hi! My name is Ellie. Can I have your autograph and take a few pictures with you?!"

He seemed relieved and happy to see someone take an interest in him. He said, with a gorgeous smile Ellie would never forget, "Hi. My name is Ricky Martin. It is nice to meet you. I am the new member of the group. Nobody is really familiar with me yet, so I appreciate you coming to me to ask for an autograph. I recently substituted for the oldest member of the group, and to many girls it was a big disappointment that he didn't come. It is one of my first times on tour outside my country, and it is not easy for me. I am not as outgoing as the others, at least not yet—maybe because I know many girls are disappointed to see me."

"I am not disappointed," Ellie said with a warm smile. "I am glad you are here and that you are new, because now I have the chance to talk to you and get your autograph and pictures. One day, I am sure I will brag to all the girls that I met you in person, Ricky Martin!"

Ellie did not realize on that day how prophetic her words really would be!

Ellie was now eleven years old.

Kindness

Many rewards are in store for us when we act from genuine kindness, without a hidden agenda and expecting nothing in return. All it takes is for us to put ourselves in someone else's shoes.

Many times we are so focused on ourselves, on how miserable we are and how we don't have the things we need to make us happy, that we fail to realize that it is in forgetting ourselves that we find true joy. If we stop concentrating on ourselves, if we stop being selfish, doors of infinite possibilities will open. Famous motivator Anthony Robbins said, "The fastest way to create a better life is to focus on becoming a better you" and "The actions we take determine us as much as we determine our actions." If he is right, then in order to become better people, we need to take actions that will benefit other people.

Many people are living through distressing times and feel they don't have the strength to go on. We complain that the world has become a very hostile place, with wars and conflicts spreading over all the continents. We want peace and love to reign, but we feel powerless before the magnitude and onslaught of evil events. Are we just going to sit down and complain?

I read somewhere that the most selfish state to be in is deep sadness, because when we are depressed, we are only focusing on ourselves. We feel so sorry for ourselves that we dwell on everything that is wrong in our lives and we miss out on what is good. Mother Teresa used to say that when we are too busy feeling sorry for ourselves, we run the risk of becoming ungrateful. We forget about all the good things in our lives and forget how much help and love other people need.

I deeply believe that through our everyday actions we can start changing our family, our city, our country and the world. By practicing kindness, we can make a difference not only in our own lives but also in the lives of everyone who comes into contact with us. We can improve the world by spreading love, one person at a time. As we begin to be kinder, a domino effect starts taking place that travels through borders, bringing more gentleness, more smiles and more love to the world

There is a wise saying that says: "Give light, and darkness will disappear." So let's forget ourselves for a minute. By being ready to help others, we can learn to feel happy and blessed rather than depressed. Let's not focus so much on the grand plans of life; instead, let's focus on the tiny frequent moments of love and happiness we can share with each other. Let's allow the invisible force of God's love to direct us and contagiously move from individual to individual. Let's start a domino effect by shining our light on others, so that darkness may give in to light! By spreading kindness, we will be contributing to a more beautiful life for all, including ourselves. When we give to others, we give ourselves a great gift, because, as another wise saying says," Little kindnesses will broaden your heart, and slowly you will forget yourself!"

The moment we put ourselves into someone else's shoes, we see things from a different perspective and from a less selfish point of view. When we manage to do this, we will realize how much other people may be hurting in a particular moment, and it will be easier for us to help them. Every time we overcome our egos and think about others, we grow inside. And, although we must do things in an uninterested manner, doing things out of compassion and not seeking anything in return, most of the time when we put others first, there is a reward in store for us.

God has designed everything in such a way that as we go through various experiences, we learn valuable lessons and discover how much improvement we need in a particular area. He also rewards us, showering us with blessings when we unselfishly engage in an act of compassion or when we successfully learn a lesson that we were meant to learn. It is beautiful to be alive and to have the chance to grow through situations that are compassionately designed to teach us loving lessons. We have the free will to do as we please, but when we choose to do good, we will surely reap the rewards. In every situation, we must look for what lessons can be learned. We do not want to waste our precious time on this beautiful earth our Creator has so lovingly made for us.

So let's open our eyes and not waste a minute. Every time we are sure we have mastered an area such as love, compassion, kindness or forgiveness, we need to pause and reflect; surely God will show us there is still much room for improvement. It is in our everyday experiences that we are able to realize, no matter how good we thought we were in a particular area of our lives, there is much we can still improve. We must not get discouraged or lose heart. And we should not be too tough on ourselves, but always remember that God is patient with us and so we should be patient too. There will always be another chance to put into practice what we have learned and to improve whatever area is still a challenge for us.

The more effort we make to spread kindness, the more contagious it will become. Let's sow the seed of kindness everywhere we go because, as the book of Ecclesiastes says, "In the morning sow your seed, and in the evening do not let your hand be idle; for you do not know which of the two will be successful, or whether both alike will turn out well." (Ecclesiastes 11:6) We must be kind to all we come in contact with: friends and strangers, the rich and the poor, the happy and the sad, the powerful and the humble. Kindness is something we must practice even towards animals and plants, because all living things deserve it and all living things will benefit from it—and, most importantly, because we ourselves will become better because of it. Where, when and to whom should we be kind? There is an easy answer. Seneca said: "Wherever there is a human being, there is an opportunity for kindness!"

Mother Teresa used to say that kindness enriches our lives; with kindness, unnoticed things become clear, difficult things become easy, and dull things become cheerful. The best way to start a new day is by doing something good—and by being grateful that we had the chance to do it. The kinder and the more thoughtful a person is, the more kindness he or she can find in other people. Put it to the test!

Offer kindness to anyone who might be around you by giving your attention, your time, your company, your advice, your gratefulness, your love. Mother Teresa advised us to not be satisfied with just giving money: "Money is not enough, money can be got, but people need our hearts to love them." What is an act of kindness? An act of kindness says: "I want you to be happy."

To sum up: God told us the greatest commandment is to love Him, and the second one is just as important, and that is to love our neighbor. One of the best ways we can love is by being kind. We must not let anything stop us. How often have we held ourselves back from trying something new because we were afraid? Afraid of what people will think of us. Afraid of rejection. Afraid of looking stupid. Afraid of being judged or criticized. Afraid of disappointment. Let's not be so self-conscious, because when we are, we waste many precious opportunities. We must make a commitment not to limit ourselves. When we feel fear about doing something good, we should determine to do it anyway! When we overcome the fear of reaching out to someone, people will feel our love and be healed. Mother Teresa said, "Kind words can be short and easy to speak, but their echoes are truly endless."

Wisdom to contemplate:

"Your kindness should be known to all. The Lord is near."
(Philippians 4:5)

"Do nothing out of selfishness or out of vainglory; rather, humbly regard others as more important than yourselves, each looking out not for his own interests, but (also) everyone for those of others." (Philippians 2:3-4)

Goodbye to Jelly Bean
–12–

It was a Sunday morning, and Ellie was very worried about her dog Jelly Bean. For two weeks now, he had increasingly become calm and mellow, almost as if he was sedated. He did not want to play, and most of the time he was leaving her side to go lie down. At first, she thought he was just being lazy, but a week into this change, she asked Anna to take him to the vet. And so they did.

The vet said Jelly Bean had toxoplasmosis and that it would be a matter of luck if he was going to get better or not. Ellie's eyes filled with tears; she tried not to blink so that the vet would not realize she was crying. She took a big breath and looked at her beloved puppy, her companion, her best friend. She felt as if a tiger had clawed her in the stomach just above the belly button. She felt so much sadness she did not know what to say next.

Anna understood what Jelly Bean meant to her daughter, and she too, felt an immense sadness to think about Ellie losing him. “But, doctor, how could this happen?” she asked. “Are you sure about what you are saying? This dog is home next to us practically every minute of the day. We take such good care of him. I just don’t understand how this could have happened!”

"Well, it only takes a minute," the vet replied. "See, this disease most commonly comes from street cats. If you have left the dog's food or water outside even once and a cat ate or drank from one of his bowls, then that is all it takes. I am sorry."

Jelly Bean was lying on his side on the vet's table. He was breathing with difficulty and looking at Ellie with his big brown eyes full of love. It was almost as if he was saying, "Don't worry, Ellie. Everything is going to be OK. Don't be sad, my little friend. You cannot help me. It was not your fault. It is just my time."

Ellie took him in her arms and lovingly transported him to the car. Ellie and Anna drove in silence for most of the way home. Anna knew exactly how Ellie was feeling, and she did not know how to make it better…she thought she should let Ellie be the first one to talk.

Ellie was lost in her thoughts. She was going to do everything in her power to help Jelly Bean get better. She was sure there had to be a mistake. "Doctors are humans, and humans make mistakes. I know there is a chance he is wrong about this. I just know it," she thought to herself and silently tried to hold back her tears.

Before they got home, she turned to Anna and said, "Mom, this can't be happening. He's wrong, isn't he? He made a mistake. Jelly Bean will start getting better any time now, right, Mom? Right?"

Anna felt a big knot in her throat. She could not swallow. "Ellie, we just have to stay as calm as we can, because you know Jelly Bean gets stressed when you are stressed and sad when you are sad. He is very sensitive to your emotional state. So you have to make an effort for him, Ellie. I know this hurts, and I know what he means to you, but you have to be prepared in case the doctor is right."

Anna was desperate to say something that made sense to her daughter or that would make her feel better, but it was so hard! Anna swallowed hard and continued. "Ellie, throughout life, we all lose people and animals we love, best friends and family members. You just have to be strong and remember that usually the reason why we feel sad when someone or something we love dies is a selfish reason. We hurt because we are going to miss whoever has died. But death is something we all have to deal with because it comes to all of us someday. We all have a different time, some sooner, some later, but we all will die. Be strong, Ellie. Please be strong."

It had been two weeks since that conversation, and even though Jelly Bean had gotten slowly worse and worse—he was laying down most of the time now—Ellie still had hope.

Reuben was worried about Ellie, and in order to distract her, he suggested a day out in a beautiful national park about an hour from the city. They would have a picnic, and that would take Ellie's mind off her dog, at least for some time.

The day was nice; the weather just perfect for such a plan. They hiked and enjoyed the clean air and the landscape. They found a perfect spot for the picnic and had a wonderful lunch. At about 5:00 p.m., they headed back home. Reuben was happy. At least, Ellie had been able to enjoy herself for the day. He missed her cheery disposition—lately, she had been so sad.

They arrived home, and Ellie immediately had a bad feeling. She could sense that Jelly Bean was not OK. She did not wait for her dad to pull into the driveway; she got out half a block early and raced to the garage, to the spot where they had left Jelly Bean. It was dark, but she could see him lying down, as he had so often in the past few weeks. To her shock, as she approached him, she realized he was not breathing. When she touched him, her hands no longer felt his cotton ball softness; instead, she felt a rigidity that would haunt her for a long time. Jelly Bean was dead.

Love of animals

When it comes to animals and love of animals, in my opinion, people are divided into two classes—those who are able to experience a profound love for animals and those who can't and therefore don't understand the first group. My comments about this last chapter will probably be understood by the people who at least once in their lives have loved an animal, be it a horse, a cat, a dog or any other pet. The other group, those people who have yet to have a special relationship with an animal, will probably just think I am crazy—but hopefully they will begin to understand those of us who deeply love animals. And maybe they will be more patient and understanding when they see someone who has lost a dear furry friend.

Some people think animals are animals and they are not meant to be loved, just enjoyed or used for work. Some people believe animals lack the capacity to love and to feel the same emotions humans do. I am not a scientist, and I have not done thousands of hours worth of research about this topic, but I have had many pets, and I have spent long hours with them. Here are my observations.

Animals have an immense capacity to love us, to forgive us, to understand us and to remain next to us no matter what. My relationships have been with dogs, but I know that the type of animal does not matter;

thousands of people are able to enjoy the love of intelligent animals of different species all around the world. The Bible says that animals were made for our companionship and enjoyment, and this is what I believe. And because they are creatures created by God, we must take good care of them.

In my opinion, being able to love and be kind to an animal is the first step to being able to love a human being. After all, animals are vulnerable, they never answer back, they do not have a concept of revenge, and they always forgive and forget. If we are not able to love such a creature, one that is always ready to love us and to receive our love, then how do we expect to be able to love a human when humans are much more complicated beings?

The pain that comes from the death of a furry friend is real and deep. When we lose a pet, we need people who are important to us to understand us and give us their support and their love. So, next time someone you love loses a pet, please remember Ellie, and understand that even if you don't feel the same way about animals, there are some people who do, and they are in desperate need of your love and understanding.

A pet can be a confidant to us, a best friend, a companion, our playmate, our pal. When I think of my dog and I try to describe him, I find it impossible. He is a very special creature that God put on this earth for me to take care of and enjoy and love. He is precious to me. When I am sad, he cheers me up; when I am scared, he makes me feel safe; and when I am lonely, he is my great companion. He has been by my side for a very long time, and he holds a very special place in my heart. It will be very hard for me on the day I have to let go of him, the day I am asked to say goodbye.

Animals never judge us, not by our actions, by our looks, by our personality or by our economic situation. All animals want and care about is for us to love them. If you have not yet had the wonderful experience of owning and loving an animal, I advise you to give it a try. An animal will unlock feelings you never knew you had. Watch programs on animals and/or wild life, or read some books on this topic and learn about animal behavior—it will surprise you. Go ahead, because loving animals is a way to start loving our world, and caring for animals is a way to start caring for our environment. Take the first step, and don't be afraid. The experience you go through when you love an animal is worth the pain you will feel when you lose the animal.

We are often too fast to see the dark side of the world. There is so much to love, so much to enjoy, so much to share. Embark upon the adventure that it is to love an animal, and you will see that there are many more sweet moments in life in store for you if you just open your heart to them.

Wisdom to contemplate:

"The LORD God said: 'It is not good for the man to be alone. I will make a suitable partner for him.' So the LORD God formed out of the ground various wild animals and various birds of the air, and he brought them to the man to see what he would call them; whatever the man called each of them would be its name." (Genesis 2:18-19)

"Ever since the creation of the world, his invisible attributes of eternal power and divinity have been able to be understood and perceived in what he has made." (Romans 1:20)

Growing Up
–13–

Ron was a very handsome, cool but shy type of boy. He was tall, and he had dark brown hair and penetrating dark brown eyes. His eyes reflected deep sadness, even though he tried to hide it. From the first time she saw him, Ellie could see right through him. Long before she heard the story of his mother's terrible death, she knew his life was hiding a very sad story.

His mother had committed suicide just three years earlier. Ron was in the house when she shot herself, the same house he was still living in. He now lived with his grandfather since his father had abandoned the family a long time ago.

Ellie had heard the story many times. He had not had the typical teenage life, and he was a lonely boy. He had no brothers or sisters, just one cousin named Marco. Marco and Ron had a close relationship, but Marco had lived with his grandmother ever since his parents had died in a car accident. After the accident, the stress had been so great on the grandparents that they had divorced. Marco had stayed with the grandmother, and at that time Ron lived with his mom at his grandfather's house. After Ron's mother killed herself, he kept on living at his grandfather's house, even though the grandfather was hardly ever home because he was constantly traveling for business. Ron usually would come home to his maid Maria, unlike the other boys his age, who came home to their moms.

Ellie was not sure when Ron had first noticed her. But she had seen him early in the morning riding his bike, back and forth, right in front of her bus stop. He used to pass by and stare while she waited for the school bus, but he never tried to talk to her. Soon enough, though, rumors started about how Ron was in love with Ellie. This was the first time a boy had been interested in her.

He was far from the perfect admirer; he was known as the school rebel and was always in trouble. But this was the first time a boy had his eyes on Ellie, and it felt good to know that someone thought she was special. But special was not all that Ron found her. The truth was that he was in love with Ellie's sweetness and thought she was beautiful. And so he was determined to get her attention.

Ellie did not know Ron well, but he had just transferred in to her school and had planned a party, to which he had invited her whole class. Ellie had been invited to this party, which was to take place in the very same house where his mom had taken her life. This made Ellie nervous, but everyone's excitement got to her, and she stopped thinking about it.

Ellie was not sure if Reuben and Anna would let her go, but it was her first party, and she would beg if necessary. She had never been invited to a real party before—and by real I mean the kind that starts after six p.m. Her parents did not like the idea at first, but they ended up giving in. After all, Ellie was growing up now, and they knew they would have to make some adjustments, both in the way they saw her and in the way they treated her. It was more than a challenge for them, but they understood the sand clock had been turned.

Reuben dropped Ellie off at six-thirty and told her he would be beeping the horn at exactly nine-thirty. If she was late coming out of the house, she knew she would lose any chance of ever going to a party again. Of course, "never" was a little extreme, but Reuben was tough, and Ellie knew it well enough to take him seriously. Reuben was nervous about the co-ed party and did not like the idea a bit. Ellie was his princess, and he wanted to protect her from everything, always and forever. Deep in his heart, he understood that this was impossible; his little girl was growing up, and he had to let her enjoy her age. He had to start letting her out of his protective shadow.

The party had been great, and for the first time Ellie had had the opportunity to meet Ron in person. He was a bit strange, always trying to get her attention. But it didn't bother her so much, and she thought he was much more handsome up close than from far away. Ellie did not realize that what was going on was not just that Ron liked her but that he was in love with her. That night, he made sure to tell everyone, in hopes someone would tell Ellie, so he could see her reaction. He desperately wanted to find out if the feeling was mutual, or at least if he had any chance at all.

By the time it was time for Ellie's dad to pick her up, he had asked for a kiss.

"A kiss? The nerve this guy has!" Ellie thought to herself, and, turning around, she left, almost running toward the door. Her father's car was already there. "Thank God! Some other day will be a better day for my first kiss," she thought to herself. In two seconds, she got into the car and hugged her dad, and together they drove home. Both of them were happy—and both of them were relieved!

Ellie was now fourteen years old.

The importance of obedience

One of the hardest things for parents is to accept that their children are growing up. The second hardest thing is to allow them to be free to grow up, while at the same time keeping a certain degree of discipline, so that kids know their boundaries and limits—because, regardless of what some people might think, boundaries are necessary and important in order for people to grow into responsible adults. After all, we encounter boundaries in all sorts of places and situations as we grow up and become part of a group. Society has many rules that have become official in the form of laws. These, too, are boundaries, and they govern most aspects of our lives. There are housing rules and regulations in our neighborhoods, bylaws in our cities, traffic laws on our roads and company rules and procedures in our jobs. So, the sooner we become used to having rules, the better our chances of growing into well adjusted people in the future.

There is nothing wrong with having rules. After all, we are part of a universe that is governed by laws, such as the law of motion or the law of gravity. Scientists understand and embrace this fact. We live as part of a world in which all our actions carry consequences. There is nothing we can do to avoid the consequences of our actions. If I put my hand into a fire, I get burned. If I jump into a pool, I get wet. If I eat too much chocolate, I gain weight. Yes, of course, we can grow up doing as we please, but if we do, we will surely encounter many difficult and painful times that could have been avoided. By learning about limits and following rules, we guarantee ourselves fewer hardships in the future and an easier life—much easier in comparison to how our life would have been if we ignored all the "rules." Discipline teaches us about the consequences of our actions. In life, every action we decide to take surely carries a consequence. Some things change our lives forever, so wouldn't it be better if we could learn to steer out of trouble before it is too late?

In my opinion, as a daughter and as a mother, it is as important to give freedom as to demand obedience. In every area of life, discipline is necessary. To love does not always mean allowing the person we love to grow without any structure, rules or boundaries. It takes much more love to discipline than to let someone be completely free.

Sometimes a parent will choose to take the role of the "easygoing parent" and refuse to discipline or impose any rules; this parent becomes the "cool one." Then, the other parent desperately tries to maintain an equilibrium and avoid complete chaos, and so this parent becomes the "mean one," always bringing order to the house. Of course, the "cool parent" becomes the popular one, and the "tough parent" becomes the "boring" one. I cannot stress enough the importance of maintaining an equilibrium in the house, for the good of the children and the health of the parents' relationship.

Parents are teammates, not members of opposing teams. If the children realize that their parents are on opposing teams, they will try to take advantage of the situation. And this will create tense moments between the parents, tense moments that could have been avoided. Loving is not necessarily synonymous with being soft; to love our children is to teach them to live in this world in the way in which they will be most happy and well adjusted. To love is to show our children the straight path, hoping for the best but understanding that each child is an individual and therefore will follow his or her own way. All we can do is show the best path we know, and after that we must just trust God and pray.

But if we have never even make an attempt to show our children any kind of path, then they will be vulnerable to all outside influences, both the good ones and the very bad ones. We should not fool ourselves into thinking that if we don't teach the right way to our children, they will choose the right path on their own. What will happen is that other people will show them "a way," "some way" or "their way"—and, being of such a young age, they will follow. Often it will turn out to be that total outsiders—peers, movie stars, movies, magazines, professors or older friends—will be the ones who show our children "a way." And many times these outsiders will end up teaching a child, who would otherwise have been good, how to be unkind, mean, ruthless and selfish. It is no coincidence our children were born to us. God chose us to be their parents for a reason. We were meant to teach them what we know concerning God's wisdom, love and joy—and if we don't, we might be making the biggest mistake of our lives.

Let's pour a lot of good ideas into our children's heads, so at least it will balance all the bad things they already hear! Freedom is important, but so is discipline. The best solution to the dilemma of giving freedom versus giving direction would be some kind of equilibrium. It seems as if I am just stating the obvious, but sometimes stating the obvious is what really helps. When our children are growing up, we must let them enjoy their age while at the same time teaching them there will always be some rules they must abide by. We must be their coach and their guiding light in the difficult road to growing up.

God, our Father in heaven, has carefully designed a plan that will teach us wisdom, lead us to safety, protect us and give us many graces. But for this to come to pass, we need obedience. Now, how can we ever be obedient to a Father whom we don't see when we have never learned to be obedient to a father and a mother whom we do see? Obedience is a consequence of love and trust. I trust my parents because I love them and know they love me. I obey God my Father out of love and trust in His amazing love for me!

Wisdom to contemplate:

"He (Jesus) went down with them and came to Nazareth, and was obedient to them (His parents)." (Luke2:51)

"Happy those whose way is blameless, who walk by the teaching of the LORD. Happy those who observe God's decrees, who seek the LORD with all their heart. They do no wrong; they walk in God's ways. You have given them the command to keep your precepts with care. May my ways be firm in the observance of your laws! Then I will not be ashamed to ponder all your commands. I will praise you with sincere heart as I study your just edicts. I will keep your laws; do not leave me all alone. How can the young walk without fault? Only by keeping your words. With all my heart I seek you; do not let me stray from your commands. In my heart I treasure your promise, that I may not sin against you. Blessed are you, O LORD; teach me your laws. (from Psalm 119)

Many Presents
–14–

Ron finally mustered the courage to ask Ellie to be his girlfriend, and she said yes. In the beginning, she just wanted a boyfriend in order to be more like a regular teen her age—many of her friends already had boyfriends. She wanted to feel like she was more grown up. Ron had pursued her so long and showed so much interest that she decided to give him a chance. He was crazy about her. He would travel abroad, and on his return he would bring all sorts of gifts to Ellie.

"But, Mom, I love the stuff he brought me." Ron had dropped a pile of gifts at her house when Anna was out shopping with Ellie. "I love the bikini and the dresses—and look, Mom, he even got me my favorite perfume. Please, Mom, let me keep them." Ellie just could not understand why Anna was so negative about the idea of her keeping the gifts. "After all, a gift is a gift. You accept it gracefully and enjoy it a lot!"

"Ellie, please understand. I always try to please you if I can, and you know I go to great lengths to see you happy, so then when I say no to something, you should realize that there must be a good reason! Don't you think?" Anna told Ellie that it was wiser to politely say no to Ron's gifts. The reason had something to do with guys getting too comfortable after girls accept their gifts.

Ellie was still pouting. She hated the idea of returning the gifts.

"Look, Ellie, you know I wouldn't say no unless there was a good reason, you know I love you, so please trust me, and please don't look so unhappy," Anna said. "Why do you think you are so unhappy?"

Ellie didn't know why she felt so unhappy about not keeping the gifts. After all, these were all things she was sure her parents would get her if she really wanted any of them.

She kept on thinking and came to the conclusion that it was not so much that she liked the things themselves. It was more about how the things made her feel about herself. The things were a symbol of how much she was liked by someone. They made her feel important, and they were proof to her peers that Ron really cared for her. She felt silly after she realized what a big deal she was making about this issue and decided to share her thoughts with her mother.

"Ellie, we cannot live our lives trying to always prove something to people. We cannot let the outside factors in our lives dictate who we are. Do you understand? See, when we let something be the measure of how special or how valuable we are, we are setting a trap for ourselves. Do you know why, Ellie? Because we will never feel satisfied, we will always feel that we are falling short of what people expect from us. And do you know why , because in reality we were made for so much more. We were made in the image of God to share in His own blessed life and to be heirs of His eternal happiness. Of course nothing in the world will ever make us feel satisfied, only God and His love for us can satisfy us."

Ellie looked at her nails and thought about what her mom was saying.

Anna continued, knowing her daughter was listening to every word. "We will always feel that what we have obtained is not a good reflection of who we are, and for this reason we will not appreciate the job, the person, the family, the house or anything else that we have. When we are trying to show people who we are by the person we go out with and trying to feel important because of how we think someone makes us look, we might end up being cruel to the person we are dating, even without meaning to. Maybe we will criticize the way he looks, dresses, laughs or dances—and thus hurt his feelings."

Ellie curled her hair between her fingers while she pensively listened to her mom's wise words.

Anna continued. "We must feel special because we are worthy and because we know we are special from the bottom of our heart. You are special regardless of whether you have a boyfriend who brings you gifts or not. I am special regardless of whether I have a beautiful family. Your dad is special regardless of his job. So, if one day the situation changes and we don't have one of these factors, we will still be OK, because who we are does not depend on tangible factors but on intangible ones. We cannot see these intangible factors or touch them; nevertheless, they are there. Do you understand, Ellie? Who you go out with is not a reflection of who you are."

Ellie nodded and smiled to show she understood. Ellie felt silly, but she was happy her mom had set her straight. Many times it is easy to be overtaken by emotions, which carry us away like a powerful ocean current. It was good for Ellie to have Anna to provide some balance and to help her see things from a different perspective. Ellie gathered all the things Ron had given her and packed them up. She had understood well her mom's reasons, and she felt good about the whole thing. She looked at her mom and smiled. She knew how special their relationship was.

Ellie was fifteen years old.

Appreciate people for who they are

We must appreciate what we have for what it is and not for what we think it makes us look like. Things outside of us can never make up for defects in what we are inside.

If we are not satisfied with who we are, then we can make an effort to fix it—to make ourselves a better person. If we can be honest with ourselves and acknowledge our defects, then we can start getting rid of them. The best way to get rid of a defect is to replace it with a virtue.

Virtue means right conduct.[5] *It comes through hard effort and, of course, through asking for God's grace. A virtue becomes part of who we are as we develop good habits*[6]*—such as thinking before we act, consciously trying to make the best choice in a particular situation, examining our motives/intentions and thinking about the consequences of our actions. We can learn virtue by reading the Bible, by listening to good advice from someone we know is wiser than we are or by reading a good book—and then acting on*

---

[5] Peter Kreeft, "Justice, Wisdom, Courage, and Moderation: The Four Cardinal Virtues", *Back to Virtue* (San Francisco, Ignatius Press, 1986), pp. 59-70.

[6] Iain T. Benson, "Values and Virtues: A modern Confusion"

what we learn. Thus, virtues are habits that give us the power to do what is right.[7]

On the other hand, if we look around and focus on the defects in the country we live in, the community we share, the institutions we want to belong to or the people we love, if we spend our time complaining about the things we want to change in these other people, we will end up unhappy and probably alone. Sometimes we might not be doing it on purpose. Unconsciously, we might feel better about ourselves if we take attention away from our shortcomings by focusing on the shortcomings of others. But if we continually act this way, we will always end up in conflict, scaring away and hurting those around us.

Sometimes we think we have fallen in love with someone, and shortly afterward the person changes (gains weight, loses a job, gets a haircut, etc.). Suddenly, we no longer feel as in love as before. We start harassing our partner and blame it on the change. Without realizing it, we become cruel, and furiously we start trying to make our partner change back into the person we had chosen. The other person gets hurt. We might not realize why we are doing what we are doing, or even that we are doing it, but slowly we drive our partner away. Eventually, we find ourselves alone or in a relationship in which love is no

---

[7] Tim Gray, "The Virtuous Life is Worth Living: Real Men Choose Virtue", Catholic Education Resource Centre. http://catholiceducation.org/articles/religion/re0368.html

longer present. And all of this is because we are looking for a "perfect person" who will surely show everyone how great we really are. We must be great, since we landed such a great catch! Right? Wrong! What a big mistake! In the end, with this attitude, everyone loses, everyone gets hurt.

Sometimes we want to belong to an organization or a club or maybe even a church, but we don't quite fit in. Then we go to great lengths to prove to the organization that the problem is theirs—because, of course, we refuse to accept that the problem is ours. It is much easier to point fingers and accuse the outside world of how it has failed us than to look inside and face how we have failed ourselves. We would rather find a million excuses than come face to face with our "ugly side."

We need to learn to come to terms with our "ugly side," our defects. Instead of denying we have them, we need to overcome our defects and say goodbye to them. We need to be honest with ourselves and be able to analyze ourselves as if we were an onlooker. Then we can look at our defects and do something about them because we will realize our defects are only a temporary part of our personality. They are only ours as long as we decide to keep them. Our defects are nothing more than potential areas of improvement, and if we look at them as opportunities to change and grow then we will not get down and depressed about them. They do not have any power over us, and they do not determine who we are—unless we allow them to.

We also need to understand that this holds true for others as well. We need to learn to dislike the defect, the bad action, the ugly behavior—but not the person. We need to see that the behavior can change and that the bad action can serve to teach a great lesson to the person. It is the action we do not approve of, not the person. It is the defect we hate, not the person. If we all try to be more honest and gentle when we talk to each other, we can contribute to great changes in each other's lives. We will help bring out the best in others and ourselves.

We are imperfect beings seeking for perfection. We have lots of shortcomings, and until we accept this, we won't be humble, and worse of all we won't be able to accept others with their defects. We won't be able to love them as they are and for who they are, without trying to change them.

Let's pray so that we can appreciate what we have for what it is, not for what we think it makes us look like to others. Let us accept ourselves for who we really are. And let us accept and love others just as they are.

Wisdom to contemplate:

"For this very reason, make every effort to supplement your faith with virtue, virtue with knowledge, knowledge with self-control, self-control with endurance, endurance with devotion, devotion with mutual affection, mutual affection with love. If these are yours and increase in abundance, they will keep you from being idle or unfruitful in the knowledge of our Lord Jesus Christ. Anyone who lacks them is blind and shortsighted, forgetful of the cleansing of his past sins." (2 Peter 1:5-9)

"God resists the proud, but gives grace to the humble." (James 4:6)

"For everyone who exalts himself will be humbled, but the one who humbles himself will be exalted." (Luke 14:11)

Dreadful Night
–15–

Ellie was now older, and her brothers and sisters had all gotten married or gone to college, so it was only her and her parents in the house. It was a Thursday night, and Ellie had stayed home with the new maid Sonia while her parents went to a cocktail party. Sonia had gone to bed early, even before Anna and Reuben had left the house. By the time Ellie went to bed, her parents had been gone for about an hour. She had stayed in her room with her door locked, in the great company of her new dog Coffee.

She had been talking on the phone with Ron, and time had flown by. When she hung up the phone, she got into bed but kept her light on to read a book. Coffee was lying in the bed and as usual was half awake and half asleep. All of a sudden and without warning, the doorknob on her bedroom door started turning as if someone was trying to come in. Almost at the same time, Coffee jumped off the bed and darted toward the door barking angrily, just as she did when there was a stranger at the main entrance door.

Ellie felt chills through her spine. She was terrified. The knob was being forced again, left and right, as if someone was determined to come in. Ellie did not know what to do, she froze. She was completely frozen. She called, "Mom...Dad...are you back?" No answer. The knob stopped turning. Ellie called again, this time louder, "Mom, Dad, are you back?" No answer. Coffee was furious; all this time, she had not stopped barking at the door, determined to scare away whoever the intruder was.

Ellie called Coffee to the bed. The dog hesitated but ended up obeying; she made her way back to the bed and in one jump landed on Ellie's lap. Ellie quickly grabbed the phone and called Ron. Suddenly and without warning, just as she was telling him what had happened, the doorknob started moving again. She knew now that she had not imagined it; it was clear that there was someone trying to come into her room. Coffee broke free from Ellie's arms and returned to her spot in front of the door, furiously barking at whatever or whoever was behind it.

Ellie called again, praying that in fact it was her parents. Perhaps they had not heard her asking who it was the prior time. "Mom …Dad…please answer me. Is that you?" The knob stopped turning.

Ron told Ellie to open the door and see who it was. But Ellie was terrified, and she could hardly move, never mind open the door. Ron told her he would come to her house and wait outside for her parents to come home, guarding her bedroom window.

"Ellie, go ahead and open the door so you can see who is there," Ron said. "Maybe it is Sonia. Maybe she is just playing a joke on you. Come on, Ellie. I am here next to you. Besides, my house is just a few blocks away, and I can be at your house in no time."

Ellie agreed to open the door. Just to get herself to stand up and move toward the door was a huge struggle. She had never felt so much fear. Her heart was beating so fast it almost hurt. Her hands were shaking, and there was nothing she could do to stop them. It was as if her body had a mind of its own and it was terrified.

She was praying with all her heart to Jesus, praying for His protection and for her parents to come home. With Coffee by her side, she stood next to the door and tried to listen. Other than Coffee's furious barking, there was absolute silence. All she could hear was her own out-of-control breathing. She knew that if someone was hiding, there was no way she would be able to see that person. After all, there were two more bedrooms and two bathrooms on the second floor, and the first floor was very big.

She opened the door, but there was only absolute darkness—darkness and silence. Coffee darted to the top of the stairs that descended towards the first floor, stiffened herself and, looking downstairs, barked more furiously than before. Ellie's fear was so great she could hardly talk.

"Call for Sonia. If it is her, she will stop, and if it is not, then at least she will come to keep you company until your parents return," said Ron.

“Sonia! So…nia!” Ellie yelled. But no answer came.

“Yell louder, Ellie. Yell real loud…so that you can make sure she hears you!” Ron said.

“SO…NIA! SO…NIA!” No answer.

Suddenly, Ellie heard one of the chairs downstairs fall to the floor as if somebody had hit it and knocked it over.

“Ron, I am hearing noises. Please hurry up and come,” Ellie said, sobbing.

“OK, Ellie. I am getting out of here, and I will be there in a matter of minutes. Go back to your bedroom and lock the door,” Ron said.

Suddenly Ellie heard what sounded like the cupboard, in which all of Anna’s coffee cups hung from hooks, shaking vigorously. Ellie’s tears were now sliding down her cheeks. Fighting her terror, she grabbed Coffee and darted into her bedroom. She slammed the door shut and quickly locked it. She felt a bit relieved to be back in her bedroom and behind a locked door, but her fear was out of control.

All of a sudden, there was a “Tak tak tak…tak tak tak.” It was the doorknob again. She could see it moving…then it stopped.

Ellie darted to her window and was ready to get out of the house, when she saw Ron’s car and at the same time, to her relief, her parents’ car. She was relieved, but she could not stop herself from sobbing. Reuben and Ron searched the house together. They found the fallen chair but nothing else. Sonia claimed she had not heard Ellie calling for her. She said she had fallen asleep listening to the TV—maybe that was why she didn't hear.

They never found an answer for that night. Anna always wondered if Sonia had been the one responsible, in an ill attempt to scare Ellie. Ellie never forgot that night, and many things happened later in that house. She remembered what Lala had said to her and hoped that it was not true. Ellie did not know then, but she would have many more scary and unexplainable experiences throughout her life. She would have to face her fears…she would have to defeat them.

Focus on where you want to go

Fear can be our worst enemy, whether it has a real foundation or it has been invented by our mind. Fear can be disabling, leaving us motionless and unable to function. It can be a devastating force in our life. Our fears are very real to us, and if we do not get control of them, they will control us. Fear can cause much pain and can keep us from doing what we want to do or need to do in a particular situation. Fear is something that we must conquer, and until we do, we will be vulnerable to its attacks, which often come when we least expect them.

There are many sources of fear. People can inflict fear on us regarding a particular thing we want to accomplish, such as getting a job, getting married, having a baby or trying something new. Fear can also be created in our heads about particular situations, such as our relationships, our job or our health. Fear can also be more abstract, such as fear of one day getting hurt in an accident or fear of having our home invaded by an intruder or even fear of the unseen.

Regardless of their cause, all fears should be treated the same. The best way to beat our fears is by facing whatever is scaring us and by having faith—faith in God, faith in our capabilities and faith in the people we love. Faith is the opposite of fear, and when we have faith, we can break free from fears.

It is only when our eyes are kept on Jesus that we can face and overcome any kind of obstacle. Remember that when Peter was walking on the water toward Jesus, he was safe as long as he was looking at Jesus; but when his eyes focused on the storm instead, he began to sink. Immediately, Jesus grabbed him by the arm, rescued him and said, "O you of little faith, why did you doubt?" (Matthew 14:31)

The Bible says that "There is no fear in love, but perfect love drives out fear because fear has to do with punishment, and so one who fears is not yet perfect in love." (1 John 4:18) Sometimes fearful situations can be an opportunity to make us understand that our relationship with God is not where it should be. If we loved Him as we should, we would not be afraid; we would trust Him completely and absolutely in every situation.

Let us keep our eyes on Jesus. Let's cast any and every doubt out of our heads. We must know in our hearts that, no matter what the situation, God will see us through! Maybe fear is wake-up call for us to eagerly desire to come closer to our God. The Bible reminds us of Christ's saving power: "He rescued us from such great danger of death, and he will continue to rescue us; in him we have put our hope (that) he will also rescue us again." (2 Corinthians 1:10) If we remember these words when fear overtakes us, then we can set our eyes on Him and not on the situation or our circumstances. We can confidently call upon His name and know He will answer us and He will protect us.

Wisdom to contemplate:

"The lamp of the body is the eye. If your eye is sound, your whole body will be filled with light; but if your eye is bad, your whole body will be in darkness. And if the light in you is darkness, how great will the darkness be." (Mathew 6:22)

"Even when I walk through a dark valley, I fear no harm for you are at my side; your rod and staff give me courage." (Psalm 23:4)

"I sought the LORD, who answered me, delivered me from all my fears."
(Psalm 34:5)

"God is our refuge and our strength, an ever-present help in distress. Thus we do not fear, though earth be shaken and mountains quake to the depths of the sea." (Psalm 46:2-3)

Is this Love that I'm Feeling?

–16–

Sometimes Ron would call Ellie late at night and tell her to look out her window. She would quickly go to her window, and there he would be—like a crazy man, standing on his car, pretending to sing and dancing to the song "Big in Japan." It was all for Ellie…all just to make her smile and to show her how much he loved her. He gave her love letters every other week, went to her bus stop in the morning and recorded tapes full of love songs. In a nutshell, he was doing everything he could to make her see that he was crazy about her.

Ron was now sixteen. That was a young age to be driving around, but his grandfather was always trying to compensate for the terrible experience Ron had witnessed by giving him all his wishes and wants. Therefore, at sixteen, he had his own car, a used white Honda Accord. Ellie was never allowed to ride in the car with him. Anna and Reuben said it was just too dangerous, and while this was true, they also felt that boys could just not be trusted.

When Ron kissed Ellie for the first time, Ellie was transported to another world. She had never been kissed before, and she had only seen it happen in the movies. He was very tender, and from that moment on Ellie was sure she would never want to meet anyone else. "He is the one. I am in love. This is what it feels like…I am sure I am in love!" she thought, with an unshakeable conviction in her heart.

Ron used to say he would marry her as soon as they were twenty-four, because he was sure they where meant for each other. He told her all his plans. He was sure she was the girl of his life. How little they knew, how little Ellie knew, that everybody has felt this way about his or her first love, but the first love is not always the one.

Anna looked at Ellie, who was looking out from the balcony daydreaming. Ellie's chamomile tea had gotten cold as she had gotten lost in the swirls the spoon was making while she gently mixed it.

Anna knew Ellie had a crush on Ron, but she was not sure how big the crush was. She did not want Ellie to be someone who was so eager to fall in love that she would fall for anyone, just because the idea of being in love is so beautiful. She knew that those who fall in love with love easily get thunderstruck—and can easily get hurt.

"My love, do you want me to warm up your tea?" Anna asked with eyes that overflowed with tenderness.

"No, thanks, Mom. I guess I just don't feel like drinking it anymore."

Anna approached her and sat by her side.

Ellie, playing with a cube of sugar, asked her, "Mom, do you think that love can last forever?"

Anna smiled and said, “True love can last forever. The key is to know if what we feel is really true love. The best way to go about it is not to rush, convincing ourselves that the first time our heart skips a beat for someone, that person must be our one true love. True love is worth waiting for, and only time can reveal to us if the love we think we feel is love indeed.”

Anna paused. She was worried that Ellie would think she did not understand her, but she continued: “Sometimes people fall in love with being in love, with the idea of being in love. They love the attention, the love songs, the whole idea of having someone special who cherishes them not because that person has to but because that person chose to. This is dangerous because it can cause a lot of confusion and often a lot of heartache.”

Ellie looked intently at her mom and wondered if she was in love or in love with love. How would she ever know? How would she find out?

Ellie was sixteen years old.

So how do you know who is the one?

I have been asked the question, "How do you know who is the one—your soul mate, your other half, the person who completes you, the one you are meant to be together with for the rest of your life?" First of all, we have to pray and try to discern if marriage is something that we are called to—because in life not everyone is called to marriage. Some people are called to witness to Christ by living a chaste single life. And others are called to the religious life; many people dedicate themselves solely and exclusively to spreading the good news of Jesus; they give themselves up for the glory of God and for the sake of His Kingdom. We can be single and happier than we ever imagined because when we live the calling God has for us – then we are truly happy.

Now, if we do feel we are called to marriage, then we should take every possibility for a relationship very seriously. It is also important for us to think and consider what things are important to us. When we are young, there are many times in which we feel that we are in love, so things can get very confusing. It is hard to advise a teenager, or anybody else for that matter, about love and about how to find "the one." After all, it is not as if we come to this world tagged and all we have to do is find the tag that matches ours. No, it is very hard to find the right mate, and we must understand that we will make mistakes—and this, of course, translates into us having to go through many heartaches and disappointments. Yes, many people have had their hearts broken a few times before they found "the one."

Before we can even begin to think about who it is that our heart longs for, before we can think about finding our soul mate, we need to make sure we have first found the absolute love of our lives—God. Only after we have a deep relationship with God can we begin to discern what He might have planned for us. God has wonderful plans of prosperity for each and every one of us. Once we find Him and we give our lives to Him, then, with His guidance and grace, we can start to look for our soul mate. Remember what the Bible says: "But seek first the kingdom (of God) and his righteousness, and all these things will be given you besides. Do not worry about tomorrow; tomorrow will take care of itself." (Mathew 6:33-34)

Now, having said that, let's continue to try to tackle the question at hand: How do we know who is "the one"? Well, although it is very hard to know who is "the one," it is easier to know who is "not the one." We must have a clear idea in our heads of what traits we just cannot accept in that person whom we could potentially fall in love with. We must know the "absolute nos." We must have criteria for what characteristics are just not acceptable to us, but we need to be realistic and honest with ourselves. For example, for some, it might be a person who:

- *Is aggressive or shows any kind of harsh behavior toward us or toward other people*
- *Drinks too much, does drugs and/or frequently gets into trouble*
- *Cheats or refers to the opposite sex in a disrespectful manner*
- *Is too much of a flirt with other people*
- *Treats us badly in front of others or humiliates us*
- *Only tells us our defects, frequently trying to put us down*
- *Lies*
- *Has major psychological problems*
- *Has no values: steals, breaks the law, deals drugs, engages in extramarital sex, etc.*
- *Is not physically attractive to us*
- *Is very different in cultural background, social background, economic status, etc.*
- *Practices a different religion or has no belief in God*
- *Has priorities very different from ours*
- *Makes his job his main priority*
- *Wants attention at any cost*
- *Humiliates and disrespects others*
- *Annoys us often*

This is not discriminating against anyone or being prejudiced against someone. We can have someone as a friend, we can be there if that person needs us, but we can decide not to date that person. If we find things about a person that we feel we cannot live with, and we do not want to deal with such things in a long-term relationship—or even for the rest of our lives—then we must try to avoid a situation that could bring us to the point of no return.

It is not a good idea to get into a relationship, especially a marriage, thinking that we are going to change the other person. Before a relationship starts, before we make a decision that might affect the rest of our lives and the lives of those people around us, we need to discern if this is a person we want to date or not.

There is an old saying that one reason marriages do not work is because in the beginning women tend to pretend to be something they are not in order to please the guy. For example, a woman might pretend to like sports when in reality she doesn't. Men, on the other hand, show themselves pretty much as they are. For example, some men flirt with every girl they see even if they are dating someone else. When they decide to get married, the man goes into the marriage hoping the girl will not change, while the girl goes into marriage sure she will be able to change the man through her love. So, the girl soon changes, and the man never does. Needless to say, the marriage fails.

There is nothing wrong with knowing what we can tolerate and what we cannot tolerate in someone who could become our spouse, nothing wrong with knowing what we can live with and what we cannot. We need to determine how much we can compromise in a particular area and in what areas we just cannot compromise. From the beginning, we need truthfulness, with ourselves and with others. If we are not honest, we are setting ourselves up for failure and unhappiness. No honesty—no success.

This way, we can pray about the matter more effectively, because it is good to be specific in the prayers we lift up to the Lord. If we want to find our soul mate, we need to ask God for His Help. He will gently guide us and will help us find that special person. He will make sure that we do not stay with the wrong one. And He will give us the wisdom and the strength to discern in every situation what is the best thing to do. From Him and only from Him can we have true hope, so that even when we feel hurt and disappointed, we can know that somewhere out there is our true love.

I know a woman who prayed to God for her soul mate and made a detailed list of all the characteristics that she thought he should have—he should be kind, gentle, faithful, committed, truthful, etc. Then she even drew a picture of him! Six months later, she met him. Today they have two children and have been married for more than ten years! So, trust in God, and know what you want.

Now, but we need to be very careful. At the same time, we can not limit God or try to boss Him around. We need to be open and have faith. With a humble heart we need to understand that we do not know everything and that God by His love and grace can change anyone. So we need to leave room to the possibility that maybe we do not know what is best for us, or who is best for us. We need to trust God completely and know that He can change anyone including us, and that He has a perfect plan and purpose for our lives although we might not completely see it or understand it at different points in our lives. If we limit ourselves by a set list of qualities, especially when that list includes physical attributes or certain personality traits like: funny, outgoing, cool, upbeat or so many other things. Then we need to ask ourselves - am I really trusting that God knows better? Do I trust that nothing is impossible for God?

Everything is possible for those who hope in the Lord!

Wisdom to contemplate:

"Love is patient, love is kind. It is not jealous, (love) is not pompous, it is not inflated, it is not rude, it does not seek its own interests, it is not quick-tempered, it does not brood over injury, it does not rejoice over wrongdoing but rejoices with the truth. It bears all things, believes all things, hopes all things, endures all things. Love never fails." (1 Corinthians 13:4-8)

"Let love be sincere; hate what is evil, hold on to what is good." (Romans 12:9)

Time to Say Goodbye
–17–

It was a cool spring day, and Ellie was on the terrace with Anna. They were silently keeping each other company. Anna was reading the book *"A Heart full of Love"*, an inspiring book about putting our love into action, and Ellie was daydreaming while she gently swung in a wide cream-colored hammock. Without realizing it, they had killed the entire afternoon by lazily sharing some quiet time together and quietly enjoying the beauty of their garden.

Before they knew it, it was time for Reuben to come home, and they heard the front door closing. "Daddy is home!" Ellie thought lovingly. She looked toward the sliding doors that went from the terrace into the living room, and, as if by magic, there he was—standing still, looking intently at the two of them.

"Oh boy, I know that look," Anna thought to herself.

Reuben had a mixed look on his face—an intense shine in his eyes and simultaneously a worried smile on his lips. His heart was pounding briskly with a mixture of excitement and apprehension. He was about to drop a bomb that would quickly disrupt this quiet afternoon and change their lives. Even though he was getting used to it by now, he could not help but wonder if the rest of the family was getting used to it as well. Nowadays, it was easier since there was only Ellie to worry about—the rest of the children had grown up and were all in university. Thank God she was a very open-minded and positive girl. He did not worry about Anna; she was tough, and, besides, she knew it was coming. He had confidence in her strength; he looked her straight in the eyes and smiled. Then he looked at Ellie.

After a few years of living in the same city, after they had gone through the long adjustment period—just when Ellie had finally adapted, had made some true friends and was finally used to her new life—there he was standing in front of her to break the news.

"We have been transferred. It's time to move again," he said loudly, like the captain of a ship ready to raise the anchor and set sail into a sea of possibilities. He gave a small pause, and then he continued. "Please be positive. At least, this time we have hit the jackpot! We are going to Brazil!"

Ellie's face instantly fell, a prisoner of a sadness that only let her go when she heard the word—the magical word—"Brazil!" She was split between the excitement of going to live in such a magical place and the fear of once again moving and letting go of her life as she knew it. She thought about her friends and her dog. She thought about Ron and all the moments they had shared. She did not know why or how, but she somehow felt ready to go and experience her new life. All sorts of opportunities lay ahead of her! She was full of dreams and full of life!

"I am going to Brazil…" she told her classmates with a forced smile.

"Are you going to live in Rio?" asked one of the girls curiously.

"No. Actually, we are going to live in Brasilia, the capital city," Ellie answered with a bit of sadness in her voice. "We are moving in two months, as soon as the school term finishes."

"Brazil? Oh, poor you!" said the girl. "I feel so sorry for you. Your parents must not love you. At least, they don't seem to. What parents would make their children go through all these changes without caring for their feelings or even asking their opinion? Besides, I heard that Brazil is full of mosquitoes and that Brasilia is the most horrible city in Brazil. You are not even going to Rio. Oh, Ellie, you are so unlucky. Poor you!"

Ellie was shocked by the comments the girl made, and a great confusion invaded her mind. Her head was full of negative thoughts and her heart full of fear. She felt as if she had been pushed from a high balcony and had splattered onto the ground. She thanked God that it was the end of the day and that the conversation had taken place when she was getting ready to get onto the school bus.

Still, it felt like ages before she reached her usual bus stop and was able to free herself of the negative atmosphere that had saturated the bus. She carefully walked down a steep slope, trying hard not to trip and fall while she quickly made her way home. Like a fast-growing infection, the venomous words of her classmate had invaded her every cell. She was sad; she was confused; she felt depressed. She needed to unload with Anna. She needed to see things from a different perspective. Only Anna could help in such cases. "Faster…walk faster," she kept telling herself all the way to home. She opened her messy schoolbag and shuffled through it to find her house keys. "Come on. It is not so hard," she told herself. "Look for the big purple dragon keychain…big purple dragon…Finally, here they are!"

Ellie unlocked the main gate and hurried to the front door, but before she could put the key into the keyhole, Anna was already opening the door with a smile in her face. "Hello, my love," she said warmly.

"I hear you," Anna said after carefully hearing all that Ellie had to say. Ellie put a baby carrot in her mouth and chewed slowly. "Look, Ellie." Ana said. "In my opinion, there are two reasons why this girl could have said such nasty things to you…and neither reason should have the power to change the way you were feeling about going to Brazil." She intently looked into Ellie's sad eyes. "The first reason is that she is sad that you are leaving and she is saying these things in the hope that you will convince us to stay. But I highly doubt that, since you tell me you two were not so close to begin with. The second reason is that she is dying of jealousy—and this is the one that I find the most possible. You know, Ellie, you have never been a jealous girl, and this is why you usually are taken aback when a jealous person says something mean to you. My advice to you is to search deep in your heart and see if you have any doubts about how much we love you. Pay attention to the way we treat you, the way we have raised you, and honestly answer to yourself if you think we love and care for you."

"Of course, I know you love me. I can see it. I can feel it. We are a team. We all make our sacrifices, and we all receive our rewards. We are a team, and we are a family. Of course, I know you love me," Ellie said with indignation. "I know you love and care for me…but what she said still hurt my feelings. I don't know why."

"Well, it's understandable, Ellie, and pretty simple. We are human, and it hurts when someone says something harmful or full of bad intentions. We just need to unload it, come to terms with it and keep on looking forward. Do you know what I mean?"

Ellie nodded.

"Now about what she said about Brazil and Brasilia: Don't take some jealous girl's word for it. Do your own research. Look on the Internet and in the school library. Let's go to the Brazilian embassy! I guarantee you that you will find the truth," Anna said in a convincing, calm voice. "The truth is out there, Ellie. We must just make the effort to find it. We can dwell on other people's mean words, or we can make an effort to find the truth."

"But, Mom, why are people so mean sometimes? I just don't understand why she cannot be happy for me." Ellie said with frustration.

"Remember, Ellie, everybody is different. You do not know what it feels like to be her. Maybe she feels stuck here and sees no chance to ever have a different kind of life. Maybe she is very unhappy and by telling you your life stinks, she feels better about her own life. Who knows? Take this as an example of what you do not want to be like. Make sure you are always able to feel happy for others and encourage them instead of bringing them down. Do not be taken over by other people's ugliness, meanness and bad intentions, but conquer all these things with good!"

Jealousy

Mother Teresa used to say that to be kind means giving much more than material things. For example, it can mean giving a smile, offering an encouraging word and sharing someone else's joy. She also used to say that to be willing to share in another's happiness is a sign of generosity. But in order to share in someone else's happiness, we need to get rid of the jealousy that sometimes arises in our hearts.

When we are jealous, we are unable to feel happy for others, and many times, instead of giving a compliment or praise, we even end up spoiling another person's happy moment by doing or saying something mean. Jealousy is a disease that sometimes creeps inside us without us realizing it. It arises from insecurity and fear, and it is often the cause of many other negative emotions and attitudes, such as gossip, resentfulness, rivalry, ill will, etc. If we are not careful, jealousy can mutate into envy, and envy into hatred, so that we even feel joy at the misfortune of others.

How do we know for sure if what we feel is jealousy? Do a self-check! If we have a feeling of sadness, even if it is slight or deep inside, at the sight of another person's material or personal achievement, then we have been bitten by the jealousy bug!

Where does jealousy come from? It often comes from pride—we think we are better than others and that we deserve more than they do. Other times, it is the result of our insecurity—we desire to have what is not ours, and we unjustly want what rightly belongs to another.

How do we stay away from this dangerous virus? For starters, we must be honest with ourselves. We need to be constantly checking if there is even the slightest trace of jealousy inside our hearts when others are more fortunate, richer, thinner, more successful, more beautiful, more loved, more popular, healthier or happier than we are. There are some questions we can ask ourselves so we don't fall into the jealousy trap: Am I bitter about someone else's good fortune or success? Do I always try to keep up with my neighbor? Do I criticize others so that they will lose confidence in themselves and so that I will look better? Do I keep comparing myself to others? Am I always looking for praise from others, and if someone else receives praise, does it bother me? Am I slow to thank, to encourage or to praise? Am I able to feel genuine happiness when someone else gets something I wanted?

We need to keep in mind that for us to be happy about our own lives, we do not need to prove that other people's lives are miserable. For us to have faith in our own path, we do not need to prove someone else's path is wrong. For us to be secure, we do not need to make someone else insecure. We need to make an effort to learn to be more humble, more self-confident and less afraid. We need to banish envy and jealousy from our hearts by desiring and exercising good will.

An old proverb says that happiness shared doubles. I believe this is true. Why? Because when we rejoice with those who rejoice, celebrate with those who celebrate and are glad for those who are glad, our reasons to be happy in life multiply! Being able to celebrate a loved one's good fortune gives us a reason to feel happy even when our own lives are not going so great.

Let's seek to always share one another's joy, because this will make us better people. It will strengthen and encourage us. And it will help us feel happy no matter what. If we rejoice in other people's progress, we will immediately feel uplifted ourselves. If we let other people's successes be our successes, others' blessings will be our blessings, others' joy our joy. So, be happy for your coworker's promotion, your colleague's new car, your old school friend's good-looking spouse, your friend's growing business, your cousin's scholarship! A person who is able to feel happy for others is able to be happy most of the time.

Wisdom to contemplate:

"You shall love your neighbor as yourself." (Mathew 22:39)

"Rejoice with those who rejoice, weep with those who weep. Have the same regard for one another; do not be haughty but associate with the lowly; do not be wise in your own estimation." (Romans 12:15-16)

"Let not kindness and fidelity leave you; bind them around your neck; Then will you win favor and good esteem before God and man."
(Proverbs 3:3-4)

The Love Letters from CJ
–18–

Ellie was now in high school. She and her family had been in Brazil for a year, and things were running smoothly. She was happy at her new school, the weather was always great, and Brazilians had a way of always being cheery, displaying a "Tudo bem!" ("Everything is OK!") kind of contagious happiness and attitude toward life. It was easy to be happy in the land of samba and sun. People were indeed very nice, and the city was quite different from anything she had ever seen. The houses had been built along a huge lake that was the focal point of the city. Most of the houses were designed to give people a grand life, with pools, huge gardens, barbecues and volleyball and tennis courts. It was the perfect pool party atmosphere! It was very easy to get used to it, and it was very easy to have fun in a grand way—the Brazilian way!

In high school, Ellie fell in love…again. How it happened she did not know. One minute she had no one, and then, all of a sudden, like a lightning bolt striking, a boy came into her life to shower her with love and attention. He was sweet and charming and knew how to talk. He was romantic and funny. No wonder he won her heart so fast. They called him CJ, and he was very popular in school, being friends with almost everybody. He was involved in most of the school activities, from the drama club to the soccer team. His mom was a funky hippie who talked about topics Ellie had never discussed before. They listened to Simon and Garfunkel and Janice Joplin. CJ's CD collection was his pride and joy. Ellie was listening to music she had never even heard of. Tracy Chapman became a favorite, and every time CJ and Ellie were together, they listened to "Sorry" and fell more in love.

Because CJ had many friends and everybody liked him, Ellie was able to meet more people and make some new friends. The first time he asked her to be his girlfriend, they were at a party, and from that day on, they were inseparable. On their one-week anniversary, CJ wrote Ellie a letter she would keep forever…nobody had ever written to her anything so special:

That thing called love is a very crazy thing…

Suddenly, when we least expect it (why does it always have to be like this!), it comes. It does not even give a warning, but, in the blink of an eye, it invades us, floods us, drowns us…it is that strange feeling that does not allow me to think. It is that which does not let me sleep. It's what makes my eyes shine and my hands sweat at the slightest encounter with yours—those beautiful blue eyes of yours that shine just as much. I am lost. I have fallen headfirst—yes, I am diving into the pool of your being. I am refreshed by your love. I am not afraid because in my heart I know that this feeling, this craziness my life has become when I am not next to you, is totally right since it has happened with the right person—you, my love, you! Loneliness? I no longer know what that is. I miss you even when I am by your side—what an addiction! This week...it already seems like it has been a month. Help! I love you so much. Where is it going to stop?! May it be eternal while it lasts! I adore you!

Happy one-week anniversary,

CJ

The love of a teenager always feels like the love you will feel for the love of your life. But even though CJ was a romantic—there was no doubt about that—he was sort of a free spirit. They were very different. CJ had been brought up with few rules and many freedoms. Ellie, on the other hand, had been brought up with discipline and rules. CJ made her think about things she had never thought about, and he challenged her individuality, her ideas and her thoughts.

One day, CJ had to go on a two-week holiday to San Francisco in California. This was his first trip out of the country.

Ellie was sitting on a kitchen stool, carefully dropping bits of chocolate chip cookie dough onto a baking pan, when she heard the dog barking. "The mailman!" she said, and in a dash she was opening the front door.

"Good morning, Ellie. No school today?" said the mailman in his usual way.

"Nope," she said while anxiously waiting for him to sort through his bag, looking for their mail.

"Here you go, darling, a letter for you. Wow! All the way from San Francisco. Lucky girl! See you tomorrow, Ellie."

Ellie's hands were holding the envelope at eye level. "Yes!" she confirmed with a smile. "It's from CJ." In a hurry, she went to sit under a tree, ripped the envelope open and started to read:

I am so glad I had not given you this card before! Now that I am finally going to send it to you, it comes to have its real value. I bought it when you went away on holidays and the days started getting longer and seemed gray even though we were on vacation and the blazing summer sun was shining outside. Everything seems so gray without you. Only you give color to my life!

I feel that the gray San Francisco days perfectly match the way I feel inside. I struggle through the endless days that I have to endure without you. I miss the everlasting days that are colored by your beautiful smile, that smile of the greatest girl in the central plains of my beloved country.

That same girl is the source of the colors of my life, the girl who creates the rainbow of happiness that now lives in me. You illuminate this rainbow from its different angles and give true meaning to its seven colors. Every day that passes, these colors are getting stronger. No, I will not let two miserable weeks apart make my heart turn gray. There's nothing I can do but give in to this love I feel. There is nothing I can do but dream of you, my Ellie, my love. Before we realize it, at the violet outburst of a morning, I will come back to look for you and take you to live with me in my rainbow. Wait for me, OK?! I left, but I am coming back!

Burning red for your love,

CJ

A few days later, Ellie received a second letter. It read:

Happy Valentine's Day! Today it is Valentine's Day, and to me it seems as if this whole country is asking me: "Where is your Valentine?" Well, the answer is: at home...one continent away from me, thousands and thousands of miles away!

This card is an expression of how on the outside I can seem like I could live without you...but on the inside, well, things become much more complicated. I could live without you...for, say, twenty minutes (like the card says)...but I would have a sad face just like the one the bear on this card has!

I so much wish that you where here with me, enjoying all of these things, seeing and learning all of this with me. And it is a bit strange: every time that I separate from you, I feel that time passes ever so slowly. And every great thing I see or do I wish I could be seeing it and doing it with you. Maybe one day it will be so! California is beautiful at this time, everything full of hearts, stuffed animals, candy and such things. And today, especially today, all of these things remind me of you. I miss you, and I love you a lot. Oh how I truly love you Are you the love that I have been waiting for? Sometimes I think I am dreaming, and then I see you in my arms and I feel lucky and scared all at the same time. May it last forever while it lasts!

Love u,

CJ

Ellie thought she had been in love before. She thought about her first love, and she remembered how she had been sure that was the real thing. But, then, how…how could this be? Could she be feeling something even stronger now? She had been sure she would marry Ron. She had dreamt of it. She had honestly thought that he was the one. And when she had left, she had been brokenhearted and had thought she would never be able to find someone else.

Nobody understands how strong the feelings of a teenager are. People do not acknowledge those feelings as love. Ellie knew adults would think of her as just another silly teenager. "What an exaggeration! Love? Nonsense!" Anna would say. So, what was she feeling? She was confused. What is love? Was this love? She just knew it was so strong that she could not eat, she could not concentrate in class and all she could talk about was him.

Six months had passed since CJ's return from his trip to San Francisco. It was time for graduation and the senior trip. The prom, too, was just weeks away. CJ was in the mood to party with his friends and to be a social butterfly. He had changed and was very cold and uninterested in Ellie. Ellie could not understand the change. He was barely calling, and he was avoiding her. Finally, one day, she confronted him and asked him what was wrong. He made it appear that she was being needy and pushy, and he told her she was exaggerating. He said that it was graduation time and he did not want to feel as if he was in chains—he wanted to have fun.

They were sitting at a picnic table in front of the soccer field. It was the end of the day, and there was nobody around because the buses had already left and almost everybody had gone home.

"Ellie, I 'm sorry. I just need some time," he said. Then he took his backpack and walked away.

She quickly grabbed her bag and followed him, since he was giving her a ride home. There was absolute silence in the car until almost halfway to Ellie's house.

Then, Ellie could not take it anymore. She burst out, "But your letters…you said so many things…you told me you loved me!" She was barely holding on to the heavy tears that clouded her eyes.

"Ellie, I am an actor. I was telling you the truth at that moment, but come on, Ellie, we are too young. Surely you did not think it was going to last forever, did you? I never lied. I always wrote 'May it last forever while it lasts.'" CJ said it coldly, almost as if she had aggravated him.

Ellie felt as if her insides where being torn apart. She was so sad. "CJ, please…what do I need to do for us to go back to the way we were?" Ellie was putting all her pride aside in a desperate attempt to fix things.

"Ellie, I need some time, OK? That is it…and you are scaring me. You take things too seriously. Now I am really confused. I am going to drop you home."

Ellie got out of the car and ran sobbing into the house. A few days later, she found out that at the senior party CJ had kissed Marla, his old girlfriend. Ellie was crushed. She had thought he loved her. She had believed his words. She had thought he would be "the one."

Anna held her in her arms and caressed her lovingly.

"Mom, I don't understand…" Ellie said miserably.

"Ellie, you may feel it is big love now, but one day you will see it was nothing compared to real love," Anna responded.

"But, Mom, I thought this was it…How do you know who is the one?" Ellie said.

"Well, my love, do you remember how you felt with Ron? We talked about how the important thing is not to know who is "the one," but to know who is "not the one." Once you see that a guy is "not the one," let him go. This is the key. Because by letting go, you allow God to put the right one in your path. Think about it, Ellie. How can we ever find the right person for us if we are stubbornly holding on to the wrong one?" Anna looked into her eyes. "Don't rush things, baby girl, and do not get obstinate about anything. If you let things flow, you will always be brought towards your ultimate best, and you will have a better chance at experiencing happiness. Just trust that God loves you and takes care of you; trust that everything is perfect and everything happens for a reason."

Ellie was determined to forget CJ, and she was determined to be OK without him. She was determined to let things flow. After all, she trusted God and knew her mom had always guided her in the right direction.

Ellie was now seventeen years old.

Lies or love?

So...let's keep talking about love. How do we know when, and if, it is love that we are feeling? Many of us have thought that we were "in love" on more than a few occasions. We have been sure that "this time this is the one." At least for us girls, it starts very early; we have strong feelings and can't fight them. Like fools, all we do is think about the person who has stolen our hearts. And as soon as we are not around that person, we wonder when he will call. So we wait desperately next to the phone, dreaming of that last tender kiss. We go to bed dying of anticipation for the next school day, wondering if that special person will be there, hoping that at least we'll get to say hi.

In my opinion, "love" is no less "love" because it is in the heart of a young person; it can be as strong as, or even stronger than, the feelings we may experience when we grow older. We daydream in the same way while we listen to love songs or gaze into the sky on a starry night. We wish with the same intensity that it will last forever. We plan and dream about the same things, and then we suffer and hurt the same way when the relationship comes to an end.

So how can we tell when love is for real? I think the answer to this question is not what is most important. Are you surprised? Maybe a bit confused? Let me explain. Love is real. Love is out there for every single one of us who believes in it. What will determine if we will find the love of our lives? What will determine if we will be happy and if one day we'll be able to experience the great blessing of real love in our lives?

When we feel in love, we should not be afraid; we should just let things flow. But there are a few rules we should follow if we want to have a better chance at finding true love. First, we must be real. No acting. No role playing. Do you know what I mean? Many times we try to give a certain impression, as if we are picking a character we are going to play in a movie. We decide what type of partner we want to be and what kind of relationship we want to have without being ourselves or allowing things to happen naturally.

But if we force things in one way or another, if we pretend to be someone we are not, or if we act in some way that we normally wouldn't, then we start out without truth. And when there is no truth, there is no chance for a good relationship. We have to start our relationships with as much honesty as we possibly can. We must be honest with our partner and with ourselves. In this way, we build the foundation of our relationship on rock.

The second thing is to let things flow. Everything is perfect if we trust in God. Everything happens for the best when we allow things to develop naturally and we know in our hearts that we have been honest. So, if the relationship does not work out, even though we might be feeling immense pain, we can find the strength to let go. By trusting that things always happen for the best, we allow God to extend his loving hand to us. He wants us to find our soul mate. He wants us to find our calling in life. He wants us to be happy.

So why don't we all do this? There are many wrong reasons for why we may pick and/or hold on to the wrong person. Here are some of them:

- *We are lonely:* *We want to feel loved, special and cared for. We see couples everywhere; love is in the songs on the radio, at the movies and on the TV. We rush into a relationship because we are so tired of being alone. It seems as if we are the only one who has not been able to have a steady relationship. All of our friends seem to be married or have boyfriends/girlfriends. We feel there must be something wrong with us! Are we not lovable? We think of how our family loves us, but we think they have to because they are stuck with us. Sometimes even our family members don't love us as they should. And so we want that special someone to come along. Someone who will sweep us off our feet. Someone who will love us because he thinks we are amazing. Someone who wants to spend every minute next to us. Someone who dreams with us. And we wonder if that is ever going to happen to us. Are we good enough, lucky enough? Millions of questions start to flood our minds, questions that cause fear and insecurity, questions that lead us to make wrong choices and big mistakes.*

➢ <u>*We feel that we are getting too old:*</u> *We convince ourselves that time is running out. The funny thing about this is that it does not necessarily hit us at a particular age. We can get bitten by the "age bug lie" at any age. Once our brain believes it, that is enough. We easily fall for it and end up obsessed with the idea that by a particular age we should have found true love. If we fall for this lie, we run a very big risk of one of two things. The first one is that we can end up rushing things and settling for someone, without giving it too much thought. We are driven by the idea that we do not want to be single after a particular age, and we are terrified by the thought that we might end up alone. The second one is that we may end up in a depression because we have reached the deadline we set for ourselves and we are still alone. Last time I checked, there was no "Secret Book of Life" that tells us by what age we must be married or at what age we will find our soul mate. It is different for everyone. For each of us, it may happen at a completely different time in our lives. For some of us, it will happen in our teens, and we will marry our high school sweetheart. Others of us will experience it in our twenties, still others in our thirties, forties, fifties and so on. The important thing is not to rush and to enjoy our life as it is. Every day we live is a gift, and many things are one-time blessings, which means they will not happen twice in a lifetime. That is why, if we end up not enjoying a particular stage in our life, one day we will regret it when we realize how foolish we were and how little faith we had in ourselves and in love itself.*

- *We want to get away from home:* *Depending on our cultural background, this may be a big incentive to rushing to find a partner. But this is not the right reason, and when we do something for the wrong reason, usually things end up going wrong. We might think that by getting out of our parents' house we are going to be happy, but it might end up not being so. If our motivation for making a life with someone is to get out of the house, we will probably pick the wrong partner. And if we are with the wrong person, once we start sharing our life with that person, it will become clear that we have exchanged one bad situation for another, and at a big cost—our happiness.*
- *We lack self-confidence:* *It is very hard for our self-esteem not to be affected when everyone we know has a boyfriend or is married, everyone except us. This can be dangerous because it is in times like this that our minds can play tricks on us and convince us of many lies. We then start giving in and believing these lies, and in the end we might end up making a big mistake or becoming very unhappy. A partner does not make us a better, happier, prettier, wiser person. We make ourselves a better and happier person. Don't count on anyone else to make you feel good about yourself. It is God who can change us and transform our lives from*

the inside out, through the power of prayer. A partner cannot do this for us, and in fact many times the wrong mate can greatly reduce our self-confidence. Let's feel good about ourselves independent of other people. Let's feel good about ourselves because we are God's precious child, and because we are unique and God made only one of us. Only then will we feel good about ourselves next to someone else; otherwise, we set ourselves up for a miserable life.

- *We need some love and attention:* *We humans will do almost anything for attention and love. Actually, most of the things we do (good and bad) are in some way to get that love and attention we so much crave. But we need to focus on getting our love from the source of all love: God. God is love, and when we have invited God into our hearts, we have all the love we need. When our relationship with God is strong and it is His love that is feeding us, then we stop craving the attention of others. If we are not careful about this, we may end up accepting someone as a partner just to get love and attention. This can be a recipe for disaster. We might end up with a broken heart or end up breaking someone else's heart. Neither option is good.*
- *Our hormones are rushing us:* *Sometimes our hormones can really confuse us. We feel a rush of emotion and passion. We feel shaky and hot. We feel butterflies in our stomach. We feel so much emotion it shakes us from the inside out. But we need to be careful because we can feel these exact same feelings*

with a person who is completely wrong for us. Big passions do not equal big love. We have to try to sort things out with a cool head. Sometimes all we are feeling is a strong but temporary rush that will pass if we breathe deeply and give ourselves some time in order to think straight. Interpreting that rush as love can mean ending up with the wrong person. Be careful.

- *We feel pressure from our family: Sometimes, by trying to be a great help, our family members can end up becoming our worst problem. Consider and respect your family's opinion and advice. But do not give in to pressure and do something that you will regret later on in your life.*
- *We feel sorry for the other person: Sometimes someone can be very persistent. But we cannot accept someone as a partner only because we feel sorry for that person. How long do you think we can pretend? Such relationships don't last, and it will be much worse when we can no longer keep pretending and things start falling apart. We should always be truthful with others and fair to ourselves. We must be kind, but we must be honest too. Love is an area where lies of any kind only bring heartache.*
- *We get into a role, and we end up confused: Believing our own make-believe world, we might dive into a relationship that only exists in our imagination. We refuse to see the other person as he really is, and the situation as it really is. If we do this, one day we*

will wake up to a life that we do not want, with a person whom we do not love.

➢ *We are used to someone:* *Do you know what is worse than breaking off a long-term relationship and accepting that we have wasted many years of our life on the wrong person? What is worse is to not break up and waste our whole life. If we put off the inevitable, things will only get more and more complicated. Feelings will get stronger; marriage will happen; babies will come. We cannot allow "feeling comfortable" to steal our happiness. Love is the one area in life in which we must not settle for comfortable, for OK, for less risky, for less hassle. When it comes to love, we should not settle. We should seek true love with every bit of our soul.*

➢ *We accept a partner for any other "wrong reason":* *I could write a whole book about just this topic, but I think by now you should have gotten the point. In summary: If we believe in love, then love will be a reality for us. If we look for love, love will find us. If we are honest in regard to love, we will experience honesty in our relationships. Give love, and you will receive love! Trust in God and He will bless you with the love of your life.*

Wisdom to contemplate:

"Children, let us love not in word or speech but in deed and truth." (1 John 3:18)

"He tells the truth who states what he is sure of, but a lying witness speaks deceitfully." (Proverbs 12:17)

" Let your 'Yes' mean 'Yes,' and your 'No' mean 'No.' Anything more is from the evil one." (Mathew 5:37)

Cycle of Life
–19–

Ellie was floating in the pool, looking at the clouds and thinking about how Anna always said that life was a series of ups and downs, with good and bad times. "When you are in a bad time, Ellie, always look forward to the good time coming," she would tell her while folding laundry. Ellie closed her eyes, smiled and wondered how it was that her mother was always right.

A year had passed since CJ had broken up with her and had gone off to college. She had done some dating here and there, but she hadn't made dating the focus of her life. Anyway, Ellie did not have the courage to fall in love again. She had some good friends now, an inheritance left to her by CJ. She had two whom she considered her best friends; their names were Jana and Teresa. Jana was one of the most popular girls in her high school. She was great at sports and very friendly. She was always in a good mood, and her smile brightened the day of whoever came her way. She was a petite redhead with shiny brown eyes and perfect white teeth. She always made Ellie laugh.

Teresa was a mixture between a bohemian and an intellectual. She was very smart and liked to talk about topics that were different, at least for girls their age. She was part of the debating team and used to win every time. Teresa made Ellie want to be a more interesting person and made her want to learn about topics with more substance—the arts, literature, social justice, you name it. The combination of both friends made Ellie very happy and made her feel complete. She cherished them dearly. After all, she had always had a hard time finding a good friend.

One day, Jana had a dinner party, and she invited a guy who was known by everyone—everyone, that is, but Ellie. Alex was the son of diplomats—his father was the Brazilian ambassador to Japan. Alex had just graduated from high school and come back home to take his university entrance exams. Alex was known to be a male version of Jana. He was handsome, with an eternal tan, brown hair, green eyes and a charming smile—the typical Brazilian guy. Funny, friendly and active, Alex was friends with almost everyone in town. Ellie was excited to meet him; after all, she had heard a lot about him, since CJ and Alex had been good friends in the past.

"Ellie, come to my house early so that you help me out, and then we can get ready together. Bring your little black dress—it looks great on you!" Jana said.

"My black dress…um…OK," Ellie replied. "But then you wear yours, OK, Jana? I do not want to be the only one in a dress tonight."

"Fine…Hey, Ellie! Ask your mom if you can sleep over! See you later, OK? Bye."

Ellie hang up the phone, collected her stuff, kissed her mom goodbye and had Reuben drop her at Jana's. Ellie was thrilled because Anna had given her permission to sleep over!

The black dress looked great on Ellie; it suited her well. Her hair was now very long, and she had a nice, slim figure. She was a beautiful eighteen-year-old. After the heartache she had suffered with CJ, Ellie had preferred to stay alone. So far, she had done well by herself, and she was trying to keep things going that way. She didn't know it, but that night events would take a turn of their own. There is no stopping the inevitable!

The bell rang while Ellie was in the kitchen helping Jana's mom get some mini quiches out of the oven. Jana rushed to the door, and, to her delight, there was Alex. Jana had not told Ellie, but she was secretly hoping that Ellie and Alex would make a match. She was tired of seeing Ellie avoid romance! For her, it was more fun to think of her two best friends as a couple. Anyway, Jana loved them both, and she was sure theirs would be a match made in heaven.

It only took one look—that was enough for Alex to fall for Ellie. He thought she was just the most amazing girl he had ever seen. He had heard about her, but in person she had stunned him all the same. During dinner, he did not stop looking her way. Ellie had noticed some interest but found it hard to believe that a guy like Alex would like her. He kept on smiling at her with his eyes, nervously looking away when Ellie looked his way.

After dinner, Jana approached Ellie and whispered into her ear, "Alex said it only took one look at you, Ellie, to steal his heart! And that is the most romantic thing I have ever heard!"

"He said that?! I don't believe you, Jana! You are lying," Ellie said.

"No, I am not lying. I swear." Jana crossed her heart.

"Well, what then…" Ellie had not finished speaking when she felt a hand on her shoulder. It was Alex.

Alex introduced himself, and from that point on they talked as if they had known each other forever. He made her laugh, and it was easy talking to him. By midnight, they had been left alone on the balcony. Suddenly, there was an awkward silence. He just kept looking at her. She kept looking down…then at him…and down again. He looked at the lake that faced Jana's back balcony. The moon was reflecting its light on the surface, the water was completely calm, and everything was shimmering. Suddenly, he found the courage to draw closer to her. He gently put the back of his hand on her cheek, and then he kissed her.

Her life had taken a 180-degree turn. She had good friends who loved her and whom she could trust. And now there was Alex. She was glad she had not let herself get too sad or too scared after CJ. She had made an effort to keep her friends, and she had not closed herself completely to the possibility of finding love. It was definitely worth the risk. Maybe her heart would be broken yet again. Maybe not. One thing was clear: Anna was right that life was full of ups and downs. But the ups are so great that it is worth it to hold on through the downs. Ellie felt the joy that appreciating the simple but great moments of life can bring!

The uselessness of planning ahead

One day we are here, the next day who knows? Everything changes. Everything can always get better if we look forward to tomorrow. All we know for sure is that we know nothing about what is ahead for us; therefore, we need to trust that every change that happens in our life will be for the best. Every day is an opportunity to change our lives, every second an opportunity to leave our mistakes, our sorrows and our fears behind. It is all up to us. We can choose to look forward to better times, or we can choose to be swallowed up by overwhelming circumstances. Let's choose to have faith and to hold on through shaky times.

What use is it for us to plan five or ten years ahead? Tomorrow we might be dead—or then again maybe not. Think about job interviewers' favorite questions: "Where do you see yourself in five years? Where do you see yourself in ten years?" The fact of the matter is that we have no idea where we will be tomorrow, let alone five years from now.

Relationships might not last forever, but memories of these relationships do! Memories of being in love or of having good friends, a good teacher, a wonderful neighbor—all of these add up to the beauty that is our life. We need to live every moment fully and give our hearts completely. And when the time to say goodbye comes, we must be strong and know that we will have other chances to love and be loved. And we must keep in mind that every situation can teach us many things if we take the time to learn.

I am confident that we will find happiness if we keep an open mind and an open heart. By giving a second chance to friendship, to love, to forgiveness, to opportunities that come our way, we give a second chance to ourselves. If we live with hope and a joyful heart, we will certainly find happiness—I am convinced of this. By looking forward to tomorrow but living today to the fullest, we can ensure that we do not miss out on the best that can come into our lives.

Wisdom to contemplate:

"Do not worry about tomorrow; tomorrow will take care of itself. Sufficient for a day is its own evil." (Matthew 6:34)

"But the plan of the LORD stands forever, wise designs through all generations." (Psalm 33:11)

"Entrust your works to the LORD, and your plans will succeed." (Proverbs 16:3)

"In his mind a man plans his course, but the LORD directs his steps." (Proverbs 16:9)

"Many are the plans in a man's heart, but it is the decision of the LORD that endures." (Proverbs 19:21)

The Accident

–20–

Ellie had just had an awful fight with Alex because he had not been honest with her. In her relationships, whether with friends or boyfriends, there was simply no room for secrets or lies. Honesty was one of the things Ellie considered most important, and finding out Alex had secrets was a terrible disappointment. "How could he have hidden something so important from me?" Until then, she had never had doubts about whether she could trust him or not; it had simply been a given for her that she could.

Ellie was badly hurt—she had found out through a third person that Alex was hiding a secret from her—but it was her best friend's birthday, and she was not going to let anything spoil that night.

Jana had been very sad lately, and Ellie thought the best way to cheer her up was to go for a car ride around the city listening to their favorite music. They were already at Teresa's house, and the mood there was awful. All they wanted to do was to hop into the car and leave all their troubles behind.

But before they got into the car, Jana stopped, looked at Ellie and said she had to talk to her for a few minutes. Ellie and Jana went for a short walk around the block so that they could have some privacy.

"Ellie, you have to be extra careful. My aunt had a dream, and she told me my best friend would be badly hurt because someone who was very jealous of our friendship had made black magic against her. Ellie, you are my best friend, and I even know who made the black magic. It is Pam Soarez. She hates you, Ellie, and she thinks you stole me from her. Ellie, I am so scared. Please tell me you will be extra careful," Jana pleaded.

Ellie had to think for a while. Jana was so nervous she was hardly making any sense. After a brief pause, Ellie said, "Jana, I believe God is stronger than any black magic. I believe He protects us all the time. I trust Him. Stop being so superstitious and have some faith…OK?"

"Just be careful, Ellie…Just be careful," Jana replied.

The girls then decided to go ahead with their long relaxing Saturday night drive. They got into the car and put their favorite mixed tape on. Ellie circled around the cul-de-sac a few times, and then they took off, determined to brighten up the night. Little did they know that this was a night that would only get darker and darker.

About twenty-five minutes into their glorious ride, they were driving and chatting about their respective loves. They were driving on one of the city's widest highways, at about 100 kilometers an hour, listening to the Pet Shop Boys' song, "Where the

Streets Have No Name." Everything seemed to be getting better when, all of a sudden, out of nowhere—BOOM! A drunk driver tried to cut in front of them, miscalculated and hit Ellie's driver's side at an absurd speed.

At first, the girls did not realize the gravity of the situation. All Jana managed to say was, "Ellie, your parents are going to kill you!"

In a flash, Ellie felt the car go out of control and begin to spin. She tried hard to regain command of her car, but it was impossible—the road was just too oily from the residue left behind by the buses that used that stretch of road. Ellie's car smashed violently against a guardrail and broke right through it, falling six meters to the road that crossed beneath the highway. The car landed brutally on the driver's side. And then, after rocking softly as if swayed by the wind for a brief moment that felt like forever, it fell over and landed finally on its roof. Inside the car, there was only silence, complete silence, and terror.

Jana was unharmed except for some soreness in various parts of her body. She was on the passenger side, and the three powerful impacts had been absorbed on the driver's side...Ellie's side. "Oh my God, Ellie," Jana whispered in shock. She stared at Ellie and felt horror and panic as she realized the gravity of the situation. Ellie was covered in blood. Blood was flowing from the side of her mouth in a crimson stream. There was blood on her clothes and hands. Was she dead?

Jana unbuckled her seatbelt and looked back. Teresa was conscious and screaming in pain. There was no visible blood, but they learned later that both of her hips were broken.

Jana dragged herself out of the car through the broken front passenger window. She looked around, saw some onlookers and screamed for help. It seemed like ages until people came to their rescue.

Finally, the firemen showed up. They managed to get Teresa out of the vehicle with relative ease, but Ellie was trapped in twisted metal. It was a miracle she was alive. The driver's side of the car had been completely destroyed with the exception of a small space around Ellie. The firemen checked for Ellie’s vital signs, and though she was in very bad condition, to Jana's relief, she was still alive. But she had to be freed from the wreckage and transported quickly to the emergency room if she was to survive.

The firemen could not get Ellie out without turning the car right side up. She would get injured a bit more, but it was her only chance. A group of volunteers plus the three firemen turned the car over, and a tall fireman hurried to cut the bent metal. They dragged Ellie out, unconscious and completely covered in blood. Her body seemed lifeless. It was a scene Jana could not bear to see—she covered her eyes and started to cry.

The firemen rushed the girls in separate vehicles to the county hospital, the head fireman desperately working to save Ellie's life.

Ellie was now nineteen years old.

Painful situations can bring us together

Isn't it ironic how in a blink of an eye our whole life can change? We often have a hard time realizing how lucky and blessed we are when everything in our lives is running smoothly. In one second our life can hang by a thread, in a moment our life can come to an end—but we go about our lives refusing to think about it. It is a subject we do not want to address. We hardly ever stop to think about the frailty of our lives and about how much we need God. We end up wasting time in meaningless things and vain pursuits—precious time that could have been spent deepening our relationship with God, mending broken relationships, improving ourselves, loving more, sharing more, finding more reasons to be happy and fewer reasons to be sad.

We do not like to think about these things, but perhaps we should—because then we could be somewhat more prepared when hard times come. Oftentimes, it is when we go through hardships that we find out what we are made of. It is then that we are given an opportunity to draw on the grace God has given us, an opportunity to exercise our strength, wisdom, love, patience, kindness and faith. It is in distressing times that we really come to experience the protection and mercy of God. If we can be ready for these tough times, through prayer, then a tragedy, a catastrophe or a great tribulation can be the source of spiritual growth and some of the biggest blessings in our lives.

Sometimes, no matter how much we have prayed and how ready we think we are to face anything, when a terrible situation comes our way, we feel like St. Augustine when he wrote in his Confessions *that he was "appalled at a world that could go on as though our catastrophe had not happened." We feel drained, we feel frozen, and only hope remains.*

Many valuable lessons can be learned about hope, faith, endurance and strength. One of the greatest lessons is that the driving force behind all of these qualities is love. God has given us human beings an amazing capacity to survive the most heartbreaking moments. The great love of God that unites and that pours out from family members, friends and even strangers becomes the solid foundation that sustains us when we most need it, that great love that many times gets forgotten in the rush of everyday life.

There are many amazing stories about people who have survived adversity and found it has not only changed their lives but touched the lives of many others as well. These are people who have survived by holding on to hope. Sometimes hope is all we need in order to make it through one more day. And one more day is all we need in order to make it through the rest of our lives—because each new day brings renewed hope and a renewed understanding that God has given us the strength to endure difficult times and the courage to go on.

Hope gives us strength when adversity pushes us to the limit. In adversity, hope gives us the ability to open our eyes and see what is really of value in life. Many people's lives change forever because in hope they find meaning to their suffering. Great difficulties can pull people together, and many times great difficulties can produce forgiveness. Difficult times and problems are part of life, but it is how we choose to see these moments and how we choose to act in these times that will determine if they are in vain or not.

Wisdom to contemplate:

"Hope does not disappoint, because the love of God has been poured out into our hearts through the holy Spirit that has been given to us." (Romans 5:5)

"He rescued us from such great danger of death, and he will continue to rescue us; in him we have put our hope (that) he will also rescue us again." (2 Corinthians 1:10)

"Blessed be the God and Father of our Lord Jesus Christ, the Father of compassion and God of all encouragement, who encourages us in our every affliction, so that we may be able to encourage those who are in any affliction with the encouragement with which we ourselves are encouraged by God." (2 Corinthians 1:3-4)

Fear of the Worst
–21–

Ellie woke up on a stretcher as she was being rushed towards the emergency room. She immediately felt sick and threw up blood all over the white sheet that covered her almost naked body. The paramedics had taken most of her clothes off, so they could see what injuries she had suffered. Ellie was confused, terrified and in a lot of pain. She could not believe that this was really happening—and that it was happening to her. She was not able to talk, everything got blurry, and she fainted.

Drifting in and out of consciousness, Ellie saw blurry images of doctors and nurses racing to and from her side. She wondered where her parents were; she ached for her mother's tender love and her father's loving protection. Tears were sliding down her cheeks and mixing with the blood that streamed from her mouth. She closed her eyes and no longer felt pain, no longer heard the hustle and bustle of the emergency room.

The phone rang in Ellie's house at 1:00 a.m. in the morning. Anna jumped up and grabbed it, knowing it could not be good news. The voice on the other end was that of Jana's mom. She explained what had happened and asked Anna and Reuben to hurry to the ER in the county hospital. Trembling, Anna and

Reuben rushed to get dressed, got into the car and sped away towards the hospital.

"My Ellie…" Anna mumbled while she cried softly. "My poor Ellie."

Many images of Ellie flashed at great speed through Reuben's head. He did not know if she was dead or alive, but the thought of losing his little girl was unbearable. He felt that, without Ellie, he would fail to live. It was just too much pain to even think he might have lost his "little one."

"Is she alive?" they asked with their hands clenched together and their eyes fixed on the doctor's eyes.

"Yes," he said to their relief, "but she has been badly hurt and will be moved from the ER into the Intensive Care Unit. The first twenty-four hours will be critical."

"Can we see her?" they pleaded.

"Yes, but only one at a time," the doctor answered.

Reuben let Anna go first. He knew that in this sort of situation she was the strongest one. And he knew that it would be very comforting for Ellie to feel Anna's presence.

Ellie woke up throwing up blood again. She felt as if a giant was crushing her chest as she struggled to sit up and turn to the side of the bed. "It's going to be OK, my love. I am here. You are going to be OK," she heard her mom saying.

"Five of your ribs are broken, and your lungs were punctured by one them. This is why you feel so much pain when you throw up," said a nurse at her feet. "You bit your tongue when the car hit the ground, and that is why you bled so much from your mouth. You also swallowed a lot of that blood, and that is why you are throwing it up now. Your clavicle is broken, as well as your hand, so you will be in a lot of pain when you try to make any kind of movement. We are giving you quite a bit of pain medication, so you will have a hard time staying awake for long. It is for the pain, but also because it is better for you if you stay as still as possible."

Ellie fell unconscious again.

The next time she woke up, her mother and father were at her side. Reuben had tears in his eyes and was petting her tangled hair. The blood in her hair had dried, making it like a hard bird's nest. She was a mess.

"Can you wiggle your toes?" Anna asked. "Can you wiggle your toes for me?" She was relieved when she saw Ellie's toes wiggling back and forth. A sigh of relief also came from Reuben. She had not injured her spine!

"Your brother is outside Ellie," Anna said. "He has tried to come to see you three times, but every time he comes in, he gets sick and has to run out to the bathroom. He got so distressed and fearful about your condition he is not able to handle it well. But he is going to make a fourth attempt now. Do you want to see him?"

Ellie and her brother had had a bad argument, and Ellie had told him he was not her brother anymore. It had been almost nine months since they had talked to each other, but she really wanted to see him. Ellie shook her head yes. She was having a very difficult time talking because of her tongue and because her neck and throat were swollen from the impact.

Her brother was silently crying, and his hands were shaking as he slowly approached the hospital bed in the ICU. "Hey, Ellie…" he said with tears running down his face. "I love you, Ellie. You are my little sister, and I cannot believe how much it hurt when I thought I might lose you. Please forgive me."

They stayed silent for what like seemed like an eternity. They both appreciated the new chance that they had been given to be brother and sister. They both realized how important they were to each other. That day, their relationship was mended forever.

Ellie's friends were constantly at the hospital. One of them, Tom, gave her his inseparable driving companion, his stuffed animal called "Tom the monkey."

Ellie stayed in the ICU four days. For a while, they were afraid she would not fully recover, but on the fourth day the doctor allowed her to be transferred to a private hospital. The ride was very difficult. Every little bump on the road felt like a gigantic shock to her broken bones. The ribs only had a bandage because the doctor had said a cast is not used on broken ribs. Her hand was also free of a cast because it had been badly cut when they had pulled her out of the car and the wounds needed to be exposed to the air for faster healing. Her clavicle was another broken bone that did not get a cast. As a result, she was feeling very sharp pains with the slightest movement.

The private hospital was very nice. There was a lovely view from her room. The hospital grounds were green and full of flowers, and they looked like a park.

Ellie was happily eating some oatmeal for breakfast. She felt like new because Anna had brought a shallow plastic pan from home and carefully washed her hair. Earlier on, the nurses had come into her room with a pair of scissors, determined to cut it all off, and Ellie had begged them not to do it. The nurses thought it was very impractical to try to wash it, and it was so filthy that leaving it as it was just not an option. Anna had promised them that she would take care of it. The job was not an easy one. It took more than an hour to completely untangle all the knots and wash and dry the hair.

After the private hospital, Ellie went home, but it was a difficult adjustment. She was happy to be home, but now everything was a challenge. She could not even sit up in bed on her own; she needed the help of at least two people. She could not brush her own teeth, brush or wash her hair or even go to the bathroom on her own. It was horrible to depend on others for everything; it made her feel helpless and frustrated. She thought about the people who have suffered spinal injuries, and for the first time she began to really understand their situation—and she prayed for them. She felt blessed not to have any major injuries, and she empathized with those who had not been so lucky.

Through it all, Alex stayed by her side. Her parents even allowed him to stay in their house as long as he slept in Reuben's office.

Ellie was determined to heal faster than the doctors had estimated. After all, she was not going to change her plans to go to study in the United States. She made a great effort to start sitting up on her own, and after a month she was already walking and going to the bathroom without help. Two months later, she was getting ready to go to college. She still had her ribs bandaged, and the hand needed physical therapy, but she managed to convince Anna and Reuben that she could go. She made the case that it would not be worth losing a whole semester and that she was strong enough.

Ellie took her flight on a Monday afternoon. Her parents' hearts were in knots, but they were proud of her strength and determination.

She had had a terrible experience, and with God's help she had managed to recover and get on with her life. She had made peace with her brother, and their relationship had become closer than ever. This was enough of a reason for Ellie to feel she would be willing to go through it all again; all of it was worth it just to be reconciled with her brother.

Reuben and Anna pondered how their little girl had survived a deadly car accident. It was the second time she had been given to them as a gift. All they wanted was for her to live fully the life that she had survived in order to live, to enjoy the moments and meet the people that she was meant to enjoy and meet. They felt blessed, they felt proud, and they felt more grateful than ever before.

Rejoice always

I am amazed at how many times painful situations can change our lives for the best. I believe it is important to "rejoice always" as the Bible says (Philippians 4:4) and always be grateful to God no matter what. To rejoice means to celebrate, to be glad, to be very pleased.

As we go through life, we sometimes face difficult situations, sad moments and challenging times—moments in which what we experience is not what we would have chosen or what we had planned. For example, we can receive bad news, have to say goodbye to a friend or loved one, go through a separation, a divorce or be fired from a job. When these things happen, we find it hard to rejoice, and we might feel it is hard to be grateful to God. At these times, we need to remind ourselves of the importance of being always grateful and ask God to give us the grace to rejoice. As it says in Philippians, we need to "rejoice always"! Not sometimes. Not only when things happen as we wish. Not only when we are happy and we think the situation is fair. Not only when things go our way. No, it says "always."

It also says "Have no anxiety at all." (Philippians 4:6) This leaves room for zero anxiety, zero distress, zero sorrow, zero worry and zero fear. But we are humans, biological as well as spiritual creatures. Sometimes our heart aches, our emotions get the best of us, our brain does not understand why things have to change or why things have to be so hard. It is sometimes hard to rejoice or feel grateful. It is human to feel sad. So what are we to do? How can we rejoice always?

In the Bible, we are advised to do three things: Be grateful, pray and think about the good!

Be grateful. The Bible says we should be "giving thanks always and for everything." (Ephesians 5:20) Let's be grateful to God every day, all the time, no matter what, especially when we are not in the mood or when we are weighed down with burdens. Let's never say, "I can't be grateful for this or for that." We can feel grateful because in a bad situation we had the opportunity to learn a lesson or because within a bad situation things could always have been worse. In every situation, we can find something to be grateful for. For example, when someone we love leaves us, we can be grateful that we had the blessing of meeting that person and having had that person in our lives.

To feel grateful, we need to remember two things. First, we need to remember as St. Francis said that "nothing is ours! Great wisdom will come to us as we meditate upon this thought until we become firmly convinced of it—we own nothing. Everything has been entrusted to us for a limited time only." The chance to share our love with others is a gift from God. Sometimes we get possessive and forget that nothing is ours and everything is God's. If we have anything even for a limited time, it is thanks to His greatness, kindness and loving heart. It is a gift.

We are blessed to have all the things we treasure in our lives, all our friends, our family, our children, our opportunities, our experiences, our health, our youth, our intelligence and our skills. But when the time comes to say goodbye, when time is up, we need to let go. We need to keep the good memories, learn whatever lesson the experience left behind, grieve what needs to be grieved and then find the courage to keep on going.

When God calls for a change in our life and/or in the life of a friend or loved one, we need to be ready to lovingly say: "Yes!" Sometimes we can be like spoiled children, whose parents have taken them to Disneyland and who have a tantrum when the vacation is over and it is time to go home. Instead of saying thank you for all they have enjoyed there and appreciating how good and loving their parents were, these children have a tantrum because they want to stay longer. They disregard the precious gift their parents have given them, and they focus instead on what they can no longer have. Let's not be like spoiled children. Let's be loving, obedient children of our heavenly Father.

The second thing we need to remember in order to feel grateful in every situation is to be humble. Humble means: meek, docile, calm, submissive, obedient, soft and gentle. It is the opposite of being proud and having a big ego. It is the opposite of "I want it my way," "I don't want it this way" and "I don't like it that way." We can be excited and full of joy at what lies ahead, but we must also be detached from everything and be ready to give it up if necessary. Let's be meek and humble of heart, like Jesus (Matthew 11:29), so that we can let go when God calls us to let go.

Pray. In order to rejoice always, the second thing the Bible advises us to do is to "pray without ceasing." (1 Thessalonians 5:17). In Philippians 4:6, we are called to pray "with thanksgiving." If we are upset and ungrateful and complaining, then we are not praying with thanksgiving! Once we have a life of prayer, then we can be sure that "the peace of God that surpasses all understanding will guard your hearts and minds in Christ Jesus." (Philippians 4:7) Even if we do not understand why, even if the situation is hard to accept, we must pray and try to rejoice, and then God's peace will guard our hearts.

Think about good things. *The Bible says: "Whatever is true, whatever is honorable, whatever is just, whatever is pure, whatever is lovely, whatever is gracious, if there is any excellence and if there is anything worthy of praise, think about these things." (Philippians 4:8) We can manage our brain well and keep our emotions in check, but we need to want to do it, and we need to put effort into it. We must make a conscious choice to focus on all the good we have. We choose where we set your eyes, either on all that is good in our life or on all that is bad. If someone says, "There is nothing good I can think of right now," we should remember that there is always God's love to feel happy about. We should never say, "I cannot thank God for this" or "I have nothing to be grateful for." Instead, as Mother Teresa advised, "we should make a commitment to see every experience, whether good or bad, happy or sad, as a magnificent opportunity to do something beautiful for God." In the toughest moments we encounter, we give glory to God if we gather the strength to smile and trust and thank, even if that is all we can do.*

Wisdom to contemplate:

"And over all these put on love, that is, the bond of perfection. And let the peace of Christ control your hearts, the peace into which you were also called in one body. And be thankful." (Colossians 3:14-15)

"No trial has come to you but what is human. God is faithful and will not let you be tried beyond your strength; but with the trial he will also provide a way out, so that you may be able to bear it." (1 Corinthians 10:13)

Going to College
–22–

Sitting on the plane gazing out the small oval window, Ellie got lost in her thoughts. All sorts of things raced through her mind—Alex, her brother, the accident, her parents, her new life, her future, her friends, her dog…she felt as if she was going to go crazy. Luckily, soon enough she fell asleep. When she woke up, the flight attendant was making an announcement that they would land in Boston in half an hour. She was so nervous she felt sick. She wondered if she had made the right decision. She felt so far away from everyone who loved her.

Alex and Ellie were confident that their love could endure the distance, that it was true love and that it was not just some teenage infatuation. They told themselves they could make it and it would not be so difficult. After all, they would constantly talk on the phone, and on the holidays they would always find a way to see each other. Ellie was not afraid for her relationship with Alex. If it was meant to be, then neither the distance, the time nor anything else could diminish the strength of their love. This was the right thing to do. She just knew it deep in her heart. Being responsible, thinking about her future and going to college was the right thing to do.

Ellie cleared customs, picked up her luggage and headed out the exit doors. She did not know a thing about the city in which she had arrived, and she had no idea how far away the college was. But someone from the college was supposed to come to pick her up, and that was a relief. Taking a taxi would have been just too stressful. She did not know a soul there—once again she would have to start from scratch.

Ellie stood outside, in a place where she thought she would be more easily spotted. She had thought that the end of August was already supposed to be a bit cold, so she had worn her black jeans and a black turtleneck sweater, but it was as hot as the middle of summer. It was sunny and very humid, and she was boiling in the outfit she was wearing. It was just too hot.

The van came late. The boy driving it apologized while he explained that he had gone to the wrong terminal and it had taken him thirty minutes to find his way to the right terminal. His name was Nick, he was from Greece, he was a junior, and he was very involved in college activities. He gave her an overview of the college, and before she knew it, he was dropping her at what he said was her apartment.

The campus was desolate, and she was the only one in the housing complex called "Laneway." She got into the apartment and found to her disappointment that it was still very dusty from the summer break. It was completely empty. There were no sheets, no rolls of toilet paper, no pillows, no phone, nothing. She suddenly felt utterly alone and was overcome with a strong feeling of homesickness. She sat on a dusty sofa and cried inconsolably.

An hour passed, and Ellie realized that crying was not going to get her anywhere. She washed her face and dried it with her sleeve, then decided to change into something a bit cooler. Digging into her suitcase, she found a white T-shirt. "This will do!" she thought to herself. She needed to buy some basic things, and she definitively needed to get to a phone so that she could call her parents and tell them she had arrived safely. She knew Reuben and Anna were worried about her—especially since they knew it would be hard for her to carry her bags and do her shopping due to the fact that she was still hurt from the accident. Ellie got tired easily, and even the most basic things were still hard for her to do. Her handwriting was still very shaky.

Ellie walked towards what Nick had pointed out as the campus center. She crossed the street and hurried to the main entrance. "It is empty…what a surprise!" Ellie thought to herself. She went into the cafeteria and found a lady in a blue uniform who was counting napkins.

"Hi, madam," Ellie said softly. "I am an international student. I just arrived and need some help. Who should I look for? And where can I find this person?"

"Oh hi, dear," the lady said with a smile. "Well, you need Mr. Pollack, and he is in room 204. Go straight ahead, turn to the left, and then turn right."

Ellie thanked her and hurried toward room 204. There she found a tall man with glasses and not much hair. On the table in front of him, a placard said, "G.B. Pollack." Ellie was relieved. She told him everything, and he was very sympathetic towards her.

"Well, young lady, I am very sorry you have had such a difficult first day. I apologize. We should have been more sensitive to the needs of an arriving international student," he said with a smile. "How about if we solve your first problem by allowing you to call your parents right away, right here from my office? What do you think about that?"

Ellie could have kissed his feet at that moment. She was ecstatic!

After a heartwarming phone call home, Mr. Pollack personally took her to a big retail store, where Ellie found sheets, a pillow, a phone, etc. Then he took her to the supermarket, where Ellie got the basics—some butter, milk, juice, pasta, bread and cheese. He helped her open a bank account, and he told her that on Monday he would help her get an account for the phone company's long distance services. Then he introduced her to a few other international students who had arrived early, just like

Ellie. They were younger but would be good company until Monday, when the rest of the student body would be arriving. Mr. Pollack showed Ellie where the nearest pay phone to her apartment was located and taught her how to call collect so that she could call her parents anytime she wanted. He had been very kind to her and had saved her from losing her mind. She was very grateful, and she knew she would never forget his kindness.

That night, Ellie gave thanks to God for Mr. Pollack's help. It felt to her as if God had placed a real live flesh-and-blood guardian angel in her path when she needed him the most. She called her parents and told them about all her adventures for the day.

Anna was worried…she regretted letting Ellie go so soon after the accident.

"Mom, I am a big girl now. Trust me, and trust God! I will be OK!"

Endurance

The song says: "When the going gets tough, the tough get going!" Learning to be on our own and becoming independent is not an easy thing to do. It is up to us to overcome the obstacles we encounter throughout life. The key is to know that no one ever said it would be easy. In life, there are happy moments, and there are sad ones; tough times and enjoyable times; easygoing people and mean, difficult people; moments when we are surrounded by people who love us and lonely moments when all we have to count on is ourselves.

We cannot foresee what is coming our way, but we can plan our reactions and be determined not to be tossed around by our problems. We can make it our goal to overcome every situation with resolution and perseverance. We can try our best to find solutions instead of freezing and feeling sorry for ourselves. We need determination in our heads and strength in our hearts, so we can keep moving forward.

When we encounter a difficult situation or a challenge, we can be sure of one thing: it can be overcome if we stop, think and then act. Every step in life is an opportunity to learn and to grow. If we fall down, then we must stand up, dust ourselves off and keep on going. We can advance toward our future with confidence, knowing that obstacles can be overcome. Little by little, we can keep moving forward, progressing step by step through all sorts of situations and the different stages of our lives.

If athletes get overwhelmed by the obstacles ahead, they will never win gold. If they settle for easy limits, they will never set new world records. If they give up too easily, they will never find out how far they can go, and they will never fulfill their potential. Anyone who wants to be a world champion must look ahead, determined to endure all hardships and to meet the toughest opponents.

Anyone who wants to be the best in mathematics will seek harder and harder problems to solve. Anyone who wants to get better at scuba diving will go to greater depths and dive in more dangerous conditions—and in the greater depths find different and more beautiful surroundings. There is a hunger for challenge within us because after every obstacle that is overcome lies a reward.

Yet, often in our everyday life, we are easily discouraged. Why? Most of us accept that life is full of changes—it is full of opportunities and challenges. None of these things should cause us to give up or be so overcome by fear or discouragement that we forget that we are warriors.

Yes, we are warriors. We are here to fight the good fight. We fight against evil and against all fears, hate and depression. We fight against our own weaknesses and defects and our own shortcomings. We fight against disappointments, against humiliations and against injustice, enduring every trial and looking forward to tomorrow.

When the water has reached our neck and we find it hard to keep our feet on stable ground, we know we can always turn for strength to God our Father. He will give us the courage and strength to continue, the faith and the will to keep on trying. We must fight this fight with joy in our hearts, knowing that in all these things we have already conquered in Jesus Christ our Lord. (Romans 8:37)

Every challenge, every obstacle can be overcome with God's help, and we can be sure that we will win the gold medal. Do you know what "gold medal" I am talking about? The satisfaction, joy and peace we feel in the moment we successfully overcome whatever hard situation or trial we have faced. There is a tremendous satisfaction in knowing that we did not look for excuses or for someone to blame and we did not play the "poor me" card. Instead, we looked for God's help, and from Him we drew our strength. When we do that, God bestows on us all kinds of good gifts—gifts such as endurance and wisdom—at the very moment we need them. Next time we face a tough situation, we need to know we already have learned, struggled and conquered that situation. We have already won! Why? Because, like Holy Scripture says, "I have the strength for everything through him who empowers me." (Philippians 4:13)

Wisdom to contemplate:

"My strength, for you I watch; you, God, are my fortress, my loving God." (Psalm 59:10-11)

"The LORD is my strength and my shield, in whom my heart trusted and found help. So my heart rejoices; with my song I praise my God." (Psalm 28:7)

"He gives strength to the fainting; for the weak he makes vigor abound. Though young men faint and grow weary, and youths stagger and fall,
they that hope in the LORD will renew their strength, they will soar as with eagles' wings; they will run and not grow weary, walk and not grow faint." (Isaiah 40:29-31)

"You are my hope, Lord; my trust, GOD, from my youth. On you I depend since birth; from my mother's womb you are my strength; my hope in you never wavers." (Psalm 71:5-6)

"Behold, I have given you the power 'to tread upon serpents' and scorpions and upon the full force of the enemy and nothing will harm you."(Luke 10:19)

Obstacles to Overcome
–23–

On the first day Ellie met her roommates, they told her that there had been a mix-up and that she needed to move out of their apartment and into a new one. The thing is, Ellie had arrived earlier than any of them and already had her bed made and her clothes in the closet. It was rude and mean for them to do this to her, but they did it anyway; they did not care, not even a little bit. Ellie packed everything and dragged her suitcase down the sidewalk about twenty meters to her new apartment.

"It is OK," she thought while she sweated in the afternoon heat. "Probably I would have been miserable if I had stayed with the other girls. Maybe these new roommates will be much better for me."

That was one of Ellie's strong points and best qualities—no matter what happened to her, she could almost always find a bright side to it. As it turned out, her new roommates were very warm and friendly, and she liked the place. She quickly got settled and was happy the incident was all over. She was ready to start her semester.

Two months passed, and Ellie was getting ready to go to eat dinner. It was a cold day—at least for her, since she was originally from such warm latitudes. She had waited anxiously for a cold day to wear her new black coat along with her scarf and gloves. She was excited. It was a silly thing, but it had been a while since she had found any reason to smile, and this seemed like the perfect opportunity for her. She headed out the door towards the dining room.

The dining room was always completely packed with people. It was a big place, full of round tables that could fit about ten people each. Every table was usually full or at least half full of chatty, loud kids. As soon as she went up the stairs, some kids started staring at her and smirking. She wondered why and walked into the dining room. The place was packed, and almost everyone was sitting in groups. As she walked toward the cafeteria, she felt people staring at her and heard a few of them making jokes. It was apparently too early in the fall to be wearing winter clothes, and nobody else was wearing more than a light jacket. As always, these kids were so bored that any little thing in school was a good excuse to have some fun at someone else's expense.

Ellie managed to ignore everybody. She got a tray and grabbed herself a sandwich and an apple juice. She tried to act as if nothing was happening. She hurried out of the food court and into the dining area again. "Great…now I have to find myself a table!" she thought to herself.

Nobody even acknowledged her presence, let alone asking her to join them. It was humiliating that after two months Ellie still was sitting all by herself at a table for ten!

Ellie finished her food and started heading home. She was trying to walk faster and faster, but it seemed futile since the girls she was trying to get away from seemed to be drawing closer and closer. They were making fun of her...making observations about Ellie's clothes...giggling...whispering...laughing...pointing at her. Ellie was used to having a hard time when starting at a new school. But somehow she had hoped college would be different. "People are older in college. Aren't they supposed to be more mature? Less inclined toward allowing intrigues to develop freely?" she thought to herself.

It was not a big deal, and after a while the girls got tired of their games left Ellie alone. But it certainly did not help Ellie feel better about her whole situation.

Adapting to college had not been easy; actually, it had been a pretty brutal experience. Ellie closed the door behind her and gave a sigh of relief. She threw herself onto the bed and thought to herself, "My terrible day is finally over!" At least, that is what she thought.

When the phone rang, it was about 9:30 p.m. "Ellie, it's for you. It's Alex," said her roommate.

Ellie's day was always changed by Alex's phone calls. Just hearing the sound of his voice always uplifted her. But this time Alex was calling for a different reason.

"Ellie, we need to break up," he said in a low, serious voice.

"What? What are you talking about?" Ellie could not believe her ears.

"It is just not working out...Long distance relationships are just too hard...I feel lonely...I need to go on with my life."

"You are seeing someone, aren't you?" Ellie asked, fearing the answer he might give.

"Yes, I fell in love with someone else. It just happened. It is not like I planned it. I am so sorry."

"You said you loved me. You said it was forever. We talked about getting married...This can't be happening...You said you loved me," she said with her voice trembling.

He stayed silent, then finally said, "Look, I have to hang up. I just have to hang up."

Ellie heard the dial tone on the other end and knew that she would never hear from him again. It was just too much for one day. She needed her mom. She needed Anna.

"Mom, what kind of a day is this?" she asked Anna between sobs. "It's like some dark force is trying to finish me. I feel down, and I don't feel like doing a thing."

Anna's heart was aching with a desire to be with her Ellie. "Call a friend and get out of the apartment. Don't be alone, and don't lie down. You cannot give sadness an opportunity to turn into depression. So, wash your face, call a friend, and head out. Sometimes we just need somebody to lean on. Do you promise me?" she asked.

"I promise, Mom," Ellie answered.

Ellie hung up the phone, washed her face and called her good friend Marco. When he heard her story, he told her to come over to his place. She thought about it. Marco was one of her only friends in school, and she could not handle being alone. Besides, Anna had said that it was important to know when we need others to lift us up, and Anna was always right. So, she got ready and was out the door in no time.

Ellie needed someone to lean on for sure. It had been one of the worst days of her life. But she would live through it. She knew she would survive it like a champion. She promised herself she would succeed in school in every possible way—but for now she just needed a shoulder to cry on.

Surviving the pain

I once read in a book that life experiences can be compared to tea: the sweeter it is the more delicious it is, but the more bitter it is the more healthy it is. Easy is not always good for us, and difficult and painful is not necessarily bad. It is marvelous when someone challenges our point of view and points out what is wrong in us. It might be something that we had not found out about ourselves before, and maybe something we wouldn't have ever found out unless someone told us. We need to try to ignore the tone of voice the person used and not be frightened by the facial expression. We need to look beyond, seeking the lesson life has for us, seeing the opportunity to improve ourselves in every situation.

The more someone disagrees with us, points out our faults and touches our wounds, the better it is for us! But accepting that is easier said than done. We are also called to love our enemy—but it is not an easy thing to do. Loving our enemy is indeed difficult, no matter how the enemy presents itself. It could be a situation, a person or sometimes even our own selves. Dealing with the pain that other people inflict on us is a big challenge. Hypocrisy, betrayal, intrigue and humiliation are not easy things to deal with.

So, why do people hurt us anyway? Oftentimes, people just have a lot of darkness inside but do not want to face it. They may have a lot of sin in their lives, and this makes them bitter and blind. To face their ugliness hurts their ego, so they live in denial. They find faults in everyone but themselves, they live in conflict with others, and then in their own eyes they don't look so bad. They justify their actions to themselves and find reasons to fight with others. In this way, they convince their consciences that they are the real victims and are not at fault. They would rather be angry and look at others with disdain than face the fact that they have a defect that they need to change.

When somebody hurts us, we must make sure we do not hate the person but that we hate the action. It is as if someone has muddy clothes—we do not hate the person, but we hate the mud on the clothes. Then, if the person changes clothes (changes his or her attitude or bad behavior) and puts on clean, white clothes, the problem is solved. We need to make an effort to love the person even though we might hate the person's actions.

We can pray for the people who have hurt us, so that they may change. Maybe those who have hurt us don't have a relationship with God. Perhaps they are in the dark, not even aware of their behavior and feeling righteous when they are not. We need to try to have compassion on them because, as Mother Teresa used to say, "You do not know what it feels like to be them!" Then we can pray, "Lord Jesus, bring them to Yourself, change them, save them."

It truly makes sense to love our enemy, even though it is hard. Why? Because the more I am challenged to exercise my beliefs, the more I am strengthened in my virtues. How can we ever be sure we are truly kind or patient unless someone challenges our patience? To be more forgiving, we need a situation that calls on us to forgive. To be more humble, we need to welcome situations that will help us to get rid of our pride. What I am trying to say is that in everything God works for our good if we let Him. How do we let Him? By remembering that every situation is an opportunity for me to become a better me!

Wisdom to contemplate:

"But he said to me, 'My grace is sufficient for you, for power is made perfect in weakness.' I will rather boast most gladly of my weaknesses, in order that the power of Christ may dwell with me." (2 Corinthians 12:9)

"We know that all things work for good for those who love God, who are called according to his purpose." (Romans 8:28)

"But we even boast of our afflictions, knowing that affliction produces endurance, and endurance, proven character, and proven character, hope, and hope does not disappoint, because the love of God has been poured out into our hearts through the holy Spirit that has been given to us." (Romans 5:3-5)

"Rejoice in hope, endure in affliction, persevere in prayer." (Romans 12:12)

"Do not repay anyone evil for evil; be concerned for what is noble in the sight of all. If possible, on your part, live at peace with all. Beloved, do not look for revenge but leave room for the wrath; for it is written, 'Vengeance is mine, I will repay, says the Lord.' Rather, 'if your enemy is hungry, feed him; if he is thirsty, give him something to drink; for by so doing you will heap burning coals upon his head.' Do not be conquered by evil but conquer evil with good." (Romans 12:17-21)

Prince in Overalls
–24–

Ellie was going to be late for her Accounting 101 class. But because she was expecting a package from her parents, she went in a rush to check her mailbox to see if it had arrived. Any mail at all could cheer her up on this cold winter day. She was freezing, it was the middle of winter, and it was the kind of cold that goes all the way to your bones, the kind of cold that hits right before it snows. She had her long soft curls loose, to help her cope with the cold air that crept down her neck. She was wearing the long black coat that she loved so much; after all, it was the first winter coat she had ever owned, and it made her feel like a movie star.

Ellie rushed out of her apartment through the back door and struggled to walk fast without slipping on the icy sidewalk, like a parrot on a newly polished floor. Ellie loved New England's winter. It was all just so beautiful—everything perfectly white and peaceful. Although her college campus was stunning in the spring and summer, for her nothing was more pure and immaculate than the sights of winter! The campus looked homogeneously white, as if white chocolate frosting had been evenly spread over it, and it made her feel as if she was in a winter wonderland in absolute harmony with the world.

Just before Ellie got to the door of the campus center, she felt a rush of energy. A mysterious handsome guy walking out of the campus center grabbed her attention. He was tall, with light brown hair and gorgeous deep brown eyes. It was as if time had stopped forever in that precise second he looked at her. He looked at her in a way that made her break out into a cold sweat, and she felt ripples go down her body. He pierced her with his deep eyes. He enveloped her with his sweet smile. There was an exotic air to him, an "I don't know what" quality. He penetrated her with his eyes; it was as if he was reading her soul.

She thought he was gorgeous and kept on running. He took one look at her—one look is all it took—and fell in love. For him, there was no doubt in his mind—this girl was the one; this girl would one day be his everything!

His name was Jonah, and he was a Turkish engineering student who had just transferred from Istanbul. He was young and handsome and determined to pursue Ellie for as long as necessary. She was going to be his girlfriend—this he knew! He found out that they had a friend in common, and so he decided to make his first move by meeting her through this common friend.

One day, when Ellie was hurrying up the library stairs, she was stopped by a loud voice that called, "Ellie, wait!" It was Ted, her friend from back home, and he was with Jonah.

Ellie could not believe her eyes. She was thrilled to see Jonah again.

"Oh, hi, Ellie!" Ted said. "I'm glad you heard me. How is everything going? You big nerd, I caught you running into the library. You are planning to spend the whole day in there again, aren't you? When are you going to learn that the library is a place to be avoided at all costs, not a place where you purposely go to spend the day?"

Ellie was used to Ted's jokes. He was a funny guy who loved teasing his friends. "Well, Ted, not all of us are so lucky that we don't need to study. Some of us actually have to do our homework, you know!" she told him, as she tried to disguise the fact that she was feeling butterflies in her stomach.

"Hey, my friend Jonah here wanted to meet you. That is why I called you," Ted said with a grin.

Ellie had her hands in her pockets and was looking at her boots. She was afraid to look at Jonah. She could not believe her ears. He actually had asked Ted to introduce her to him. It took her by surprise, but she was ecstatic about it.

Jonah decided to ask Ellie out on a date, and one night they went out to the college bar. Ellie had one too many whiskey sours and got a bit tipsy, so she asked him to drop her home. That night, they kissed. She tried to tell herself that it was because of the tipsiness and to forget the whole thing. She was afraid of her feelings for him. She would avoid him and try not to think about the kiss. She would fight her feelings and ignore her thoughts. She was afraid of what she had felt with that kiss, afraid of what she felt when he was around her, afraid of what she felt when he looked into her eyes. Doubts started to invade her mind, fear of yet another heartbreak.

But a chain of events had been set into motion, and there was an imminent 180-degree change coming in her life. Jonah was more determined than ever to conquer her heart.

What was coming ahead of Ellie could not have been foreseen. Life sometimes takes us like a giant, powerful wave on the beach, without us being prepared for it or even able to resist it. Sometimes events just run their course like a river gaining strength with every turn. We cannot prepare for such events, we cannot anticipate them, and all we can do is surrender to what God has in store for us. This is part of the beauty of being alive!

Ellie was now twenty years old.

True love

We all wonder...does true love really exist? Will it happen for me? When will it happen in my life? Some of us go through life trying to appear strong and independent. Many of us go through life alone, struggling with loneliness and convincing ourselves that love is not a reality but a myth. We think Hollywood has exaggerated things and that people are fooling themselves, and we tell ourselves that we are smarter than that. We see ourselves as realistic, mature, independent and self-reliant! Besides, we are too busy, too this or too that to believe in love. After all, there are so many fish in the sea. We convince ourselves that it is illogical to think that there is only one perfect match for us and that we have to go out into the world to find him or her. It is ludicrous to think we need to put up with one person and one person only for the rest of our lives; after all, we are sexual creatures, we need variety, and times have changed! Right?

Wrong! I am sorry if I disappoint you, but I am of a very different point of view. I believe people tell themselves lies as a defense mechanism, to protect themselves. They often convince themselves of ideas that have been taught to them by their own brains, a bitter psychology professor or the media. Many times, we tell ourselves that love does not exist, so we can excuse the fact that we are incapable of commitment.

Maybe we need to face the fact that we need to change a few things about ourselves. Maybe, of all the chapters in this book, this will be the one that you will really disagree with. But look at it from the bright side—if you can discern what is good and valuable for you and ignore what is bad, then what you are reading is already worth it. If you don't like what I say but you feel in the very depths of your soul that I am right, then maybe you should reorganize your priorities and your life. Do not be afraid to change your mind!

True love is a reality, not a myth. But someone who does not believe in love will never find it. Perfect people are a myth, not a reality, but a perfect match does exist for each one of us. The idea that we can only fall in love with a perfect person is nonsense; it is unreasonable and unrealistic. But loving someone as a package, with all of his or her good and bad characteristics, is a possibility. Hoping for things to run smoothly and without any obstacles from the very beginning is unrealistic, but working things out one problem at a time is a wise approach. If two people keep in mind their love for each other and focus on the goal of being happy together, then, no matter what disagreement or argument happens, they will be able to overcome it.

This is what I want to say to you in a nutshell. Now let me be a bit more specific. The most important thing is to always be honest with ourselves. Yes, we need to examine ourselves and find out what kind of person we are, what our priorities in life are and what we want or don't want. This is essential in order for us to steer our lives into the right direction.

If, from the bottom of your heart, you know that you never want to marry and that you will be happier by yourself than with a partner, then you can skip this chapter. If you are called to live a single life, then you need to embrace that call. Those called to the single life can live very fulfilling joyful lives, lives that God uses to touch and bless others. But, if, in the depths of your heart, you know that you believe in love and you want to find your soul mate, if you feel you are called to marriage, or if you would like to understand people who do , and/or give advise to those who need it then this chapter might be a good read!

I believe we all have a soul mate. I know this sounds corny, but it does not make it less real. Many people are bullied into giving up their desire for and belief in a soul mate. But, in my opinion, there is a person out there for each one of us who will not only complete us but will also bring out the best in us, a person with whom we will become one flesh. We will no longer feel as if we are two people, but one more complete person.

Somewhere, there is a person who will force us to extend our limits and who will not allow us to ever be mediocre. Someone who, in one way or another, will propel us to continue to improve and grow spiritually. Someone who will inspire us to be more patient, kind, humble, forgiving, encouraging, giving, trusting, truthful, hopeful, enduring and balanced. The person we fall in love with will make us push ourselves to the limit. That person will help us to become a better listener, advisor and friend. Sometimes that person will lovingly correct us or remind us of what is important. At other times, that person's behavior will demand that we put into practice concepts that we believe in but have never acted on.

Finding this very special someone is not an easy task. But the best things in life don't come easy. Why are we willing to try hard, look hard and work hard when it comes to our career, making money or being beautiful—but not when it comes to finding true love?

Why? Maybe because the world often teaches us to be mediocre in our dealings with love and society pushes us to have meaningless relationships. We are told that we should "have a taste of each different ice cream." Our society applauds "not being so serious" and "having fun"—and in the end all that happens is that we end up empty, frustrated and alone.

Why do we let the world tell us what to believe? Why do we get duped into pursuing a series of meaningless relationships? Maybe because deep inside we think it is better not to believe in a great love than it is to pursue true love and never find it or, even worse, find love and then lose it. So maybe, as usual, the culprit is fear. My guess is that it is a mixture of fear, ego and selfishness. Because in order to have a great love, you have to be willing to give it everything you have and to risk everything you have for it. For a great love, you need two people who are willing to sacrifice and to compromise. In such an endeavor, there is no room for ego. There is only room for two people who have opened themselves completely to each other in order to become one, one in mind and actions, two people trying their best to endure and to overcome whatever challenges come their way.

Some people know that they are in love right away; other people take a while to realize it or to have the courage to accept it. When we are in love, it is important to recognize it, acknowledge it and act on it. With love, taking a chance is always worth it. Rejection you can live with, but missing out on the love of your life is something that is tragic and, many times, unfixable. The hardships that may come as part of the journey we embark on when we meet that special someone are worth it—because loving is a feeling, a place, a situation, an experience that cannot be matched by anything else.

To love is to choose to love. Yes, loving is a choice, a choice to make ourselves vulnerable, to not pretend, to not use masks and to give our hearts completely. To love is to believe we can love and be loved. To love is to dive into something with our heart full of trust and our mind set on the idea that we will be committed to it in good times and in bad, come what may. Loving requires constant revision of our "self." It requires second-guessing ourselves and being open to accept that there are many things we need to change and many areas in which we need to improve. This is why I say that for one who does not believe in love it will be hard or even impossible to ever experience it or even understand it.

There are no guarantees—just our faith in this love we have found and our faith in God, because God is the glue that holds the two together. He is the source of all hope, the source of all patience and the source of selfless love. God's guidance is the only way to correctly discern if what we feel is love. It is an awesome truth that one thing always remains the same—that we can always count on God for help in our every decision. When we invite God to help us decide and through prayer seek for answers, then answers will be given to us. God knows the plans that He has for us, and if we invite Him into our every situation, then each time we will be given the gift that we need in order to make the best decision. He will make sure we have all tools we need in order to make the right choice. God will help us open our eyes and open our hearts. It is His delight to help us find our way in life. If we open our hearts, we will be able to discern what is good and pleasing to Him.

Wisdom to contemplate:

"Indeed, the word of God is living and effective, sharper than any two-edged sword, penetrating even between soul and spirit, joints and marrow, and able to discern reflections and thoughts of the heart." (Hebrews 4:12)

"Do not conform yourselves to this age but be transformed by the renewal of your mind, that you may discern what is the will of God, what is good and pleasing and perfect." (Romans 12:2)

"And this is my prayer: that your love may increase ever more and more in knowledge and every kind of perception, to discern what is of value, so that you may be pure and blameless for the day of Christ." (Philippians 1:9-10)

The Auction
–25–

Ellie was slowly walking down one of the corridors in the campus center, daydreaming and playing with her hair. She had a few minutes until her next class, and was trying to kill some time to clear her head. Suddenly she stopped, her eyes fixed in the direction of the wall just before the game room. Ellie had spotted a flyer that was pinned to one of the bulletin boards on the far left of the wall.

She hurriedly approached the flyer. It was close to Valentine's Day and she was curious about what would be going on around campus. She did not have any plans yet, but was hopeful that Valentine's Day had something special in store for her. She glided towards the bulletin board and began to carefully read it.

It read:

St. Valentine's Day Auction

Come join the Student Senate Valentine's Day Auction and have the chance to take the person of your dreams out on a date. Never had the courage? Always dreamed of that cheerleader, that football player MVP or that special someone? This is your chance to show that person what he or she has been missing. The most beautiful and popular people in school will be auctioned to highest bidder. The highest bid of the night will win a limousine ride and dinner for two in the Boston Hard Rock Café! Come, participate and support the

Student Senate Valentine's Day Auction

at 8:00 p.m. in the cafeteria!

"Ellie, will you participate?" asked a female voice behind her.

Amused by the question, Ellie turned around to face Marjorie, the president of the student senate.

"Look, we need people to participate, so that we can break the record this year," Marjorie said. "You might end up winning. The prize is the best one in years. Think about it, Ellie…A limo ride to Boston is not an opportunity that should be passed up."

Ellie gave her a candid smile but declined her offer. There was no way she would go up on stage. She was not going to risk getting up in the middle of the cafeteria to be humiliated. She thought about the scenario—her going up on stage and no one wanting to bid for her. No way. There was no way she would go up there.

It was finally Saturday night, and the Valentine's auction was the talk of the college. Ellie got ready and headed towards the campus center with her three roommates. She was wearing stretch burgundy pants with a belt, a burgundy patterned long-sleeved shirt and her black coat. It was February, and the weather was still freezing. They hurried along the pathway, trying not to slip and fall. They all were looking forward to a night full of fun and surprises. When they got there, Ellie was asked one more time to go up for auction, and one more time she declined.

The cafeteria was packed with people, some sitting down, others leaning on the countertops and the rest just standing around. Jonah saw Ellie and called her over to his table. She pushed her way through the crowd to say hello. "So, Ellie, are you going up there tonight?" he asked, smiling at her.

"No way. Imagine if nobody gave a dime to go out with me. I would die of the humiliation. There's no way I am going to risk it," she said, shaking her head no.

"Look, Ellie, the prize is something I have been wanting to do for a long time. All I have to do is be the highest bidder, and that is easy. These are all college kids, and no one is going to want to bid too high. But I am willing to go as high as it takes to take you to Boston for dinner and a limo ride. So you have nothing to lose...Of course, that is assuming you'd like to go with me." He flashed her the most charming smile.

Ellie was already regretting it as soon as the words came out of her mouth: "I'll do it, Marj."

Before she knew it, she was standing on stage at the front of the cafeteria, and they were announcing her name. "We are starting the bid at three dollars. Who bids three dollars?"

A hand went up...It was not Jonah. The guy looked like someone from her Accounting class.

"OK, we have three dollars. Who bids five dollars?...Who bids five dollars?"

Another hand shot up. Ellie did not recognize this guy either, except that he was not Jonah.

The bids kept going up. "Who bids eighteen dollars?...eighteen dollars?"

Then, suddenly, she heard Jonah's voice. "I bid fifty dollars!"

Wow! She was relieved. At least, she was not going end up out on a date with some strange guy and no limo ride.

"I'll bid sixty dollars!" said another voice. She was shocked. A few "oohs" and "ahs" could be heard. It was David Carrera. David was a preppy handsome guy from senior year. He was tall and had dark hair and blue eyes. He had tried to flirt with Ellie a few times in the library, but she had forgotten all about it until today.

The bidding war for Ellie went on for a long time, until Jonah had had enough and David could not compete anymore. "Three hundred and thirty-two dollars," Jonah said firmly." People in the cafeteria were having the time of their lives. Nobody in the history of the college had ever gone so high in the Valentine's auction.

"Three hundred and thirty-two dollars going once, going twice...and the winning bid tonight is Jonah's! He wins a limo ride to Boston with Ellie—and very much deserved it is!"

Everyone cheered.

Ellie was almost ready when her roommates came to tell her that the limo had arrived. This was going to be Ellie's first time in a limousine. Jonah knocked on the door, and she opened it. He was in a gray suit, looking gorgeous and smiling at her with that irresistible smile that made her feel chills all through her body. The driver opened the limo door, and they got in. It was simply awesome. It was going to be a great night—there was no doubt about that. Before the restaurant, they stopped at a liquor store, and he bought an expensive wine to enjoy on the way back.

At the restaurant, they enjoyed their meal and laughed a lot. It was easy to be with him. He was such great company, and she felt so at ease around him. Time flew by, and the time for dessert came. "So, Ellie, what are you going to get?" Jonah asked.

"Oh, I don't know. It is so hard for me to decide. You know I have a sweet tooth. If it was up to me, I would have everything!" she said from behind the menu.

"OK, then it is very easy," Jonah answered with a grin. "Waitress, we want to order all the desserts on the menu."

"All the desserts on the menu? All the desserts? What are you, pigs?" she said very rudely.

"Please just bring all the desserts to the lady!" Jonah said, looking sternly at the waitress.

The table had eight different scrumptious desserts on it, and Ellie was thrilled. Nobody ever had done such a thing for her. It was like a scene from a movie. She did not even know which one to start with. It was a dream come true, the first of many that lay ahead.

Of course, as always, the girls in school had been bitten by the jealousy bug. On Monday morning, Ellie found out that many girls from the senior year had started some nasty gossip about her. It didn't matter. Ellie was determined not to let anything ruin her wonderful fairy tale "dream auction." After all, nothing had happened. They had returned that same night to the college and had had just one brief kiss goodnight. He had been a total gentleman, he had charmed her, and she was not able to get him out of her mind. One thing was for sure. She would not let gossip wound her heart again. She had gone through it too many times. She was determined to let it go in one ear and out the other.

"Let them gossip," Anna said on the phone. "Soon they will forget all about it, and, sadly enough, they will choose some other victim to devour with their tongues. Just ignore them, my sweet Ellie. If you have peace in your heart, then let that peace take over, because if you let them upset you with their meanness, then you will fall into their trap, and it will rob you of the happiness you deserve. That is what gossip does, my love—it robs people of peace and happiness."

Ellie, as always, gave careful thought to what Anna had said—and felt at peace with herself. "Goodnight, Mom. I love you, OK?! Don't forget that. And thank you. You always help me put things into perspective."

Ellie hung up the phone and went to bed, but not without replaying in her head the wonderful magical date she had had with Jonah!

Ellie was twenty-one years old.

Controlling the tongue

Let's focus on controlling what can become our worst enemy—our tongues. Let's say no to gossip and to all the other hurtful things that we can say to others! The people around us are very precious. When we are down, others can help us get up. When we are sad, others will cheer us up. When we feel we cannot go on, others will motivate us and encourage us. There is a proverb that says: "He who throws stones drives away birds; he who insults a friend breaks up the friendship." Nobody is an island. We all need each other, especially when we are lonely or sad. But if we scare away everyone who cares for us by misusing our tongues, then we will inevitably find ourselves very alone.

When we misuse the tongue, it harms us and others. We need to realize the importance of avoiding its bad habits. With the tongue we: lie, gossip, give away secrets and speak angry words. All these things will result in us becoming increasingly lonely. Why? Because people try to avoid pain at any cost, and lies, gossip, angry words and the betrayal of secrets hurt. Nobody likes pain, so we cannot blame people who drift away and avoid us if we have hurt them.

Sometimes the damage done by our words is obvious, and sometimes it is not. But the damage is not any less because we cannot see it. If we want loyal, caring, good friends, we have to be one ourselves. We need to be careful, so we do not lose all those people who love us. When we gossip and lie, we destroy the peace of those around us, and good people will after that do anything to avoid us. The only ones who will be left around us will be other gossips and liars, who will sooner or later end up gossiping or lying about us.

The rule is simple: If we have nothing nice to say, it's better to say anything at all. This does not mean that we don't criticize or admonish the people we love. Criticism given in love is helpful and valuable. When our intention is to help and make things better, we still need to think carefully before saying it, and if we are still convinced it is a good thing to do, we can go ahead and speak. But if we are going to say something out of anger, jealousy, envy or revenge, or when the intention is to hurt, then our words are better not said. We must always think before we talk!

The tongue can do a great deal of damage, but the tongue can also do a great deal of good—as long as it is controlled by love. Without love, nothing can bring us good, but every action inspired by love, even if it seems small and unimportant, will bring some fruit afterward. Let's make an effort to control our tongues. Any time we are trying to accomplish something of value, every time we want to do something good, we need to put effort in it. After a while, all our efforts will pay off and the results of our efforts will be good—because when a good thing is repeated several times, then it becomes a habit. Let's make it a habit to use our tongues for loving, encouraging, motivating, congratulating and everything else that is good. We can change the world, one word at a time!

Wisdom to contemplate:

"The tongue is a small member and yet has great pretensions. Consider how small a fire can set a huge forest ablaze. The tongue is also a fire. It exists among our members as a world of malice, defiling the whole body and setting the entire course of our lives on fire, itself set on fire by Gehenna...With it we bless the Lord and Father, and with it we curse human beings who are made in the likeness of God. From the same mouth come blessing and cursing. This need not be so, my brothers. Does a spring gush forth from the same opening both pure and brackish water? Can a fig tree, my brothers, produce olives, or a grapevine figs? Neither can salt water yield fresh." (James 3:5-6,9-12)

"He tells the truth who states what he is sure of, but a lying witness speaks deceitfully." (Proverbs 12:17)

"He who guards his mouth protects his life; to open wide one's lips brings downfall." (Proverbs 13:3)

The Real World
–26–

After the "dream auction date," Ellie decided to forget Jonah. She was trying to use logic in her love life to diminish the chances of getting hurt. She had thought about it a thousand times. He was one year younger than she was, and younger guys do not want to be serious. She, on the other hand, wanted to find someone who would be ready to make a commitment. Anyway, he was from the other side of the world; surely he would have to go back home sooner or later. Even if he wanted to become serious, she could not possibly move halfway around the world to a country she knew nothing about. So, Ellie decided to stay away from him. After all, she had feelings for him already, and she knew that the more she saw him the more her feelings would grow.

Then, David Carrera started wooing her, and she decided to give him a chance. He was a smart, preppy guy who was about to graduate and was a bit older than she was. It didn't really work out with him, though, and by the summer they were not seeing each other anymore.

It was a hot day at the end of the summer break, and Ellie had arrived on the college campus earlier than her roommates. She was the first one in her new campus house, and that was great. She could pick her bed—she loved the top bunk—and she could unpack slowly while listening to music.

After she had finished unpacking, she was sitting thoughtfully by the window, looking at the trees as they graciously rocked with the wind. Suddenly, Jonah's white sporty car slowly made the turn onto the road that circled the housing complex. He would pass in front of her place in a few seconds. She had the urge to see him. She could not stop herself from running out and waving at him to stop. She was wearing her pink summer dress and had her hair up in a bun. She had not looked in the mirror for hours, but she thought, "Who cares?" In a hurry, she jumped off the couch and rushed outside. He had already passed her house, but he saw her in the rearview mirror, slammed on the breaks and put the car into reverse.

Ellie was barefoot, but she didn't care. It was as if her legs had a mind of their own. The campus was deserted, and the weather was mild and pleasant. She stepped onto the fresh green grass and smiled. He was tanned, and his hair was long and golden from the summer sun. Before she knew it, they were kissing…How she had longed for this kiss!

"Give me a chance to show you I can make you happy," he said while he held her in his arms.

"I am tired of getting hurt. I am tired of trusting like a fool," Ellie answered. "I need to know that this time it is for real. All I want is to find someone who loves me and whom I can love. I want to have something more than college fun. Look, if you are this serious, if you know I am the one, then let's get engaged. Otherwise…leave me alone."

It was not Ellie's intention to rush things, but she was in her last semester, and graduation was around the corner. Knowing that she was going to have to go home in a few months, she did not want to start a relationship that wasn't going to last. She had learned her lesson about long distance relationships. She also could not make the huge decision to stay and not go back home unless it was for something huge. Yes, only something huge could keep her from going back home. Something like deciding to build a life with someone, knowing that this time it was for real. Was she rushing? She had no other alternative. If this was going to work, then it would have to be based on commitment. If he loved her as he claimed, then why not make it official, so that she could feel secure with him?

"Do you understand?" she continued. "I either go back home or stay here, but staying here is a gigantic decision. To stay, I would need to know that you are serious."

He looked into her eyes. She was the love of his life—he knew that—but getting engaged was a huge step, and it scared him. He was hesitant. But he could not think of his life without her, he could not let her go, and he knew she would not stay unless it was for something more solid than just a fling. "Stay. I know I can make you happy," he said with confidence.

They drove to Boston and looked for an engagement ring on the weekend. They found a place that specialized in diamonds and engagement rings and were led to a special room in the back, passing through various armed doors. They decided on a gorgeous diamond in a platinum setting. It was official—they were engaged! It was not very romantic, but it was surely fast and practical. Ellie looked at her ring and smiled.

After graduation, Ellie found a job with a major toy company, the second biggest toy company in the world at that time, and she was able to buy her first car with the help of Reuben and Anna. They gave her half of the money for the car as a graduation gift and said she could pay them back the rest little by little. She got herself a few suits, and she felt independent and grown up. Everything was happening so fast.

Life soon came back to normal, though. With no more plans to make, things slowly fell into a routine. Ellie was working hard and coming home exhausted from work. She woke up early and, with not much on her mind, went to sleep around ten o'clock each night.

Jonah, on the other hand, was in his senior year in college, and waking up late was a regular thing. He had been careful to schedule his first classes to start at

11:00 a.m. He enjoyed going out every night of the week.

"Why do you have to categorize days?" he asked angrily. "Who said you must do this on such-and-such a day and that on another? You should just go with the flow, Ellie. If you feel like going out, go out, and if you don't, don't. I am in my senior year, and I feel like going out when I want. You work, and therefore you are tired all the time and don't feel like going out. So don't go out. But don't ruin my senior year because you are too tired. My father is thirty years older than you, and he works in a position with a thousand times more responsibility than yours—but he still goes out and is as fresh as lettuce the next day to go to work. So, it can be done. You just do not want to!"

They were having many problems. It was not just the going out. Time was passing, the time for his graduation was coming closer, and issues started coming up.

"I want to get married. I don't want to be engaged forever," Ellie complained. "We made a decision that we would get married after graduation. But now you say that things are working just fine as they are and that you are not ready for marriage. You say that you are too young and that you need more time. You told me you were willing to live in my country, and now you are saying you will go back to yours. I cannot live in yours! I explained this to you when we were just friends and you were telling me you would move to my country for sure. I was honest with you, but you were not honest with me! I cannot move to halfway across the world. I cannot think about being so far away from my parents—you know that! On top of everything, you now say that even if we get married, you never want to have a baby. You run around, going out every night, drinking with your friends, and you are totally insensitive to whether it hurts me or not. What happened? How can someone change this much!?"

Ellie was sad, and so was Jonah. It was nobody's fault. They were just facing the stresses of different things coming together: graduation, a new job, commitment and, of course, facing the consequences of rushing things too much.

Ellie was now twenty-two years old.

Don't rush

Life passes very fast, yet all of us try to rush into things and make it pass even faster. Even if you are one of those people who think they take their time, enjoying the different stages of their lives, I guarantee you that you, too, are in some way trying to rush through life. We always desire what is ahead, convincing ourselves that if we were just there, or at that age, or with such-and-such a person, or in such-and-such a job, then we would be happy.

But every moment we live is a blessing. Every person we meet is fascinating. Every place we visit is an adventure. Every activity we engage in is a delight. Every stage of our lives is a wonder. We must become more aware of the beauty in everything we experience. If we are single, we should revel in the joy of being free. If we have a commitment, we should savor the glory and security of being committed to something or someone.

When we rush through things, we tend to miss the beauty of our surroundings, and we tend not to learn whatever it is we were intended to learn in that specific time or situation of our lives. We also forget things much more easily; we do not savor the little blessings in our lives. And it is much easier to make mistakes. When we rush through a recipe, we are more likely to end up with something unsavory or inedible. When we rush through cleaning our house, it is much easier to leave some corners dirty. It is no different with the larger issues of our lives. When we rush into making decisions, chances are we will overlook some important detail, some key factor and make a huge mistake. When we rush into getting a job or when we rush into relationships, we might be setting ourselves up for big disappointments.

Some things are too important to rush into. Good things come to us with the passing of time. A good friendship, a good wine, a good romantic relationship—they all have one thing in common, and that is that time makes them better and richer. Especially when it comes to relationships, our heart needs to be ready, and the heart of the other person needs to be ready. If not, we may go through a very painful experience. For good things to come, we need to have patience. And we need to trust that God is the one who moves and changes hearts—and we cannot and should not rush Him!

Wisdom to contemplate:

"There is an appointed time for everything,
and a time for every affair under the heavens.
A time to be born, and a time to die;
a time to plant, and a time to uproot the plant.
A time to kill, and a time to heal;
a time to tear down, and a time to build.
A time to weep, and a time to laugh;
a time to mourn, and a time to dance.
A time to scatter stones, and a time to gather them;
a time to embrace, and a time to be far from embraces.
A time to seek, and a time to lose;
a time to keep, and a time to cast away.
A time to rend, and a time to sew;
a time to be silent, and a time to speak.
A time to love, and a time to hate;
a time of war, and a time of peace."
(Ecclesiastes 3:1-8)

Losing Big Time
–27–

"The magic is gone," Jonah said, looking her straight in the eye.

"What? What do you mean?" Ellie answered in astonishment. "You said you loved me. You said I was the love of your life. You said you wanted to be with me forever. What do you mean the magic is gone?"

"I am sorry," he said softly. "I am so unhappy I cannot possibly see how I can make you happy. I need time alone. I need to sort things out."

Jonah's cousin had just passed away from cancer, and the pain of the loss was just too much for him to bear. Ben had not just been Jonah's cousin; Ben had been his best friend ever since he could remember. Ben was the best person he had ever met, and now he was dead at twenty-one. "How could God let this happen?" Jonah kept asking himself. He was so angry at life, angry at God and angry at himself for not being able to change anything that he felt as if bitterness and anger were another form of cancer invading every cell of his body.

Ben had wasted away slowly. He had suffered from brain tumors for years. After many operations, the family had been hopeful that the last operation had eradicated the cancer. But it had returned stronger than ever, and in the last year Ben had grown weaker and weaker. He had lost his hair and had lost a lot of weight. He had been so weak towards the end that he didn't have the strength to stand up. Jonah kept asking himself: Why did this happen to him? Why?

Jonah had gone to visit Ben and had not been able to recognize him. He had come back home with a broken heart. But he had still had hope—he had been told to pray, and people had told him that God surely would listen to his prayer. Then, suddenly one night while he was finishing some of his homework, the phone had rung. It was the call he had been dreading. "Ben died two hours ago…" a teary voice had said on the other end of the line." It had been his aunt, Ben's mother. At that moment, Jonah had felt his heart break into a thousand pieces.

He had made his decision, and nothing would make him change his mind. He needed to be alone. How could he ever make anyone happy when his emotions were flaring out of control? One minute, he was so sad he felt as if a black hole was engulfing him. Another minute, he was so angry he wanted to be face to face with God so he could tell Him how unfair He had been, so he could yell at Him that he did not believe in Him anymore. Ellie asked why he was so angry at God.

Jonah said: "Because God is supposed to be love. And love does not kill so mercilessly, love does not torture someone slowly until he succumbs to pain and lets go of his life. Love does not let a good person's life waste away. How could this happen?!"

Ellie remained silent, not sure what to say.

Jonah would not draw Ellie into his misery; he would not ruin her life like that. The whole experience had changed him in his innermost being; for all he knew, he might never be the same again. Anyway, he could not deal with what now seemed a trivial problem. He could not deal with their boyfriend-and-girlfriend fights. He could not deal with Ellie's demands and complaints. He needed to end it. He needed to move on and try to forget everything. He felt as if he was drowning in his own sorrow and there was nobody who could help him, not even God, not this time—he was too angry at Him. God had not answered his prayers, so he did not need Him now. Jonah felt lost; his very cells ached with the sorrow of losing someone so loved.

"You cannot push me away," Ellie said, desperately trying to convince him to stay. "This is when you need me the most."

"Ellie, I keep trying to have a picture of my life from now on, and, to tell you the truth, every time I think about this picture, you are not in it," Jonah said. It was as if a sword had pierced Ellie's heart. She made an effort to keep on listening. "I cannot possibly make anyone happy when I am this unhappy. All I will do is draw anyone around me into this sadness I am in, and that is not fair. I have made my decision. I am sorry, Ellie. I love you, but everything has changed. I am not the same anymore, and I am leaving."

"No matter how hard I try to help you, to get close to you, you just keep pushing me away from you," Ellie cried. "I don't seem to be getting through to you, to your heart—it is like you have built a brick wall around it. You don't want to share with me how you feel; you don't want to open up. I don't know what to do anymore. I cannot handle the idea of losing you. I just do not believe what you are saying. It will pass. Just give it some time, please; give it time. If you don't, you are not just going to be sad and upset, but you are going to be alone. Don't you see?" But there was nothing Ellie could do to change his mind. Jonah packed up his things and left. And just like that, it was over. Ellie felt empty and alone,

Ellie was twenty-three years old.

O death, where is your sting?

When tragedies happen, when people we love die, we tend to wonder why God let it happen, especially if death seems unfair, untimely or just plain wrong. We hurt, our heart is overwhelmed with loneliness, and we long for the person who has died. We are sure that God must have made a mistake! Our emotions fluctuate madly, from sadness to anger, from rage to depression. We develop doubts about everything we hold dear, and we feel afraid. But, worst of all, we feel betrayed by God.

In the book As I Lay Dying, *Richard John Neuhaus talks about death and about grieving. He expresses many deep truths about this topic, but there are two statements that were specially striking to me: "There is a time simply to be present to death—whether one's own or that of others—without any felt urgencies to do something about it or get over it. The time of mourning should be given its due." and "This life is now coming to an end; this life never lived before and never to be lived again."*[8]

Grieving is something we all have to go through. The more we are aware of God's love for us in our life and in our situation, the faster we will heal. Only God can and will bring healing to our heart.

---

[8] Richard John Neuhaus, *As I Lay Dying: Meditations on Returning* (Basic Books, 2002), pp. 44, 30.

"Unless a grain of wheat falls to the ground and dies, it remains just a grain of wheat; but if it dies, it produces much fruit. Whoever loves his life loses it, and whoever hates his life in this world will preserve it for eternal life." (John 12: 24-25)

"That which is corruptible must clothe itself with incorruptibility, and that which is mortal must clothe itself with immortality....Then the word that is written shall come about: 'Death is swallowed up in victory. Where, O death, is your victory? Where, O death, is your sting?'" (1 Corinthians 15:53-55)

Breaking Up
–28–

Ellie was distraught. She was used to having Jonah always at her place. After school, he would just come, make himself a sandwich and watch TV, waiting patiently until Ellie would come back from work. In fact, he used to eat most of his meals there. He would bring his homework and study at her place. Since he spent so much time at Ellie's, little by little he had brought over some of his stuff. Now that they had broken up, every little thing reminded her of him, and the heartache was almost too much to bear. She turned towards his favorite poster, a giant "Pink Floyd–The Wall" poster, ripped it off the wall and tore it into tiny little pieces.

She could not think of life without Jonah. She would go to brush her teeth, only to find a lonely toothbrush no longer in the company of its long-time companion…Jonah's toothbrush was now somewhere else, far from her. She would open the coat closet, and his half would be empty. She would look out the window, and there would be her lonely black car, no longer in the company of Jonah's contrasting white car.

When she went to bed that night, Ellie felt utter emptiness and loneliness as she thought of the new reality in her life. She lay on her bed and remembered one of her favorite songs. She started singing it in her head. The song asked if she believed in life after love. The singer seemed to have had her heart broken too and was wondering if she could be strong enough to move on. The singer had come to the conclusion that she was just too good for the guy and that indeed she was strong enough to move on. Ellie pondered these words. Was she—Ellie—strong enough? Could she move on?

Ellie missed Anna, her sweet voice, her loving advice. Ellie's heart was aching, but eventually an irresistible drowsiness took hold of her, and she fell into a deep sleep. It was a restful sleep she badly needed, since she had been crying for such a long time.

Ellie woke up and looked in the mirror. She did not recognize herself. Her eyes were swollen and red. Her hair was a mess, not from sleeping but because in her distress she had messed it up with her hands while she had repeatedly asked herself if she would be ever able to believe in love again. She was so deeply saddened by all that had happened that she called in sick to work for three days in a row. If she allowed herself to keep going like this, she was going to lose her job and lose her mind. She knew she needed help…She called Anna.

Anna, as always, listened to her beloved daughter with attention, as Ellie explained between sobs everything that had happened. Anna felt sorry for the pain Ellie was going through. Nevertheless, she felt the need to remind Ellie of a few things. She knew she needed to get her out of her "poor me" mindset.

"That is enough crying, Ellie!" Anna said sternly. "It is unacceptable to me to be hearing you as distressed as if you had been married to this man for an eternity. You were just boyfriend and girlfriend. Put things into perspective, and get over it, Ellie. Do you understand that some women have been married twenty or twenty-five years to their husband, they have had kids together and all of a sudden one day they see themselves facing a separation because their marriage has fallen apart? I know many women who have been brave and strong enough to go forward and succeed in having a happy life after they have lost everything they have cherished and loved. Changes happen, Ellie. People die, and people leave. We cannot let these things destroy us. You are a mess, Ellie. Shame on you for allowing yourself to love someone in such a destructive way. You cannot fall apart because someone has left you. It happens. You fall, you get hurt, maybe very badly hurt, but then you stand up, dust yourself off and keep on going. You have been greatly blessed by God. You have your health and the love of many people who care for you. You owe it to yourself to shake this off and keep on living. Not only that, but you must find the strength in yourself to be happy again and to believe that you can love again and be loved. The fact that some guy could not love you the way you deserve does not mean love will not happen for you. Anyway, you do not want to marry such a man. Sooner or later, he was bound to hurt you, because when he hurts, he pulls away from those he loves. Unless he changes, you cannot consider taking him back. In life, Ellie, both you and he are going to hurt many more times. Many people will die in the course of your lives, and many hardships will come your way. You need a man who will find strength in you and be a strength to you, not one who will pull away from you when the going gets tough."

Anna paused to see how Ellie was receiving the sermon. She could hear nothing. "Are you there, my love?"

"Yeah…" Ellie answered, as loudly as a mouse would answer if a mouse could talk.

"Look, Ellie, if he is the one, he'll come around. Sometimes people need time to grow inside. Sometimes they just need time to put things into perspective and give weight to those things they hold dearer. Anyway, Ellie, you two had many issues that you were not able to work out. If you want to know what I think, I think this is the right thing for you right now. Pull yourself together, and think a lot. Think about everything you have, and think about the fact that there is nothing that should shake you up in such a big way. Be strong, and have faith. God always has a plan for us. If we let Him guide us, we will always find out that everything that happens in our lives, no matter how it initially looks—good or bad, happy or sad—is for the best. Feel His loving hand in everything, and trust Him, Ellie—then your life will always be blessed, no matter what."

Ellie hung up the phone. She felt as if someone had done something very painful to her but something very necessary. It was as if an arrow had been lodged in her shoulder and she had had someone take it out. It had hurt, but it had been necessary. Talking to Anna had given Ellie an infusion of strength. She still felt lonely and sad, but something had changed inside her. She was determined to be happy. She was determined to get over Jonah and live her life. From this day on, she would stop holding on to the past and would be open to the future, facing it with a glad heart. After all, God had always taken good care of her, and she knew that this time would not be an exception.

Can you recognize yourself?

We have all gone through some tough breakup or heartache. Actually, any time a relationship ends, it is very painful, no matter what type of relationship it might have been. A traumatic experience like this sometimes causes us to act differently, and maybe we will see a side of ourselves we did not even know we had. We might act in an irrational way or say mean things. We might cry or yell. We might break things or throw things. We might even think about taking our lives. When a situation of great stress arises, when we are faced with the fact that someone we greatly loved might not love us, it is a moment of great pain. We may be so distraught that we fall into a depression, lose our job or gain more weight than we ever thought could be possible.

Unfortunately, these situations do happen, at least once in our lives. When they do, what we need to do is to find a way to come out of them, instead of drowning in our own sadness and our own self-pity. We might feel the situation was unfair. Maybe someone lied to us or used us. Maybe we feel we wasted years of our lives or we were deceived into believing something that was not true. In any case, there is no safe way to avoid such things. All we can do is not let the horrible facts control us, not let ourselves be immobilized by a situation that has no solution, at least for the moment.

We need to remind ourselves that sometimes it is necessary to let some time pass. We need time to collect our thoughts, analyze the facts and revise our feelings. We need time to heal and to get used to our new situation. We need to remind ourselves that we cannot let ourselves collapse. We need to love ourselves because if we don't, we will be no good to anyone else. If we take our lives or if we fall into a deep depression, then who can we help? Who can we love? Who can we strengthen?

We need to stick around so that we can help others live through the same types of situations and so that we can encourage those who feel sad or weak. We can be a rock to others and let them lean on us in their tough days. Helping others is always a good way to help ourselves. We need to remember that most radical changes in our lives might not only have been necessary but might also have been for the best. Sometimes we get so attached to a person that we cannot let go. By not letting go, we close the doors to happiness, because we do not allow that person to grow and we do not allow new people to come into our lives.

So what do we do if our hearts have been broken? We seek help. We turn to God and ask for His love and mercy. We pour out our hearts to Him. We allow ourselves to be healed by His loving touch. He is always there to guide us and lift us up when we fall down. If we draw closer to God, He will draw closer to us! We need to focus on deepening our relationship with Him, and then everything will slowly start improving. Only then will we be able to turn to others. That is the second thing we need to do. We need to ask for the help of those who love us...maybe a family member or maybe a good friend. We need to open ourselves up to the help that comes from God through others.

At the same time, we need to remember that God gave us a brain to help ourselves, and we need to use it. We need to think of ways to cheer ourselves up. For example, we should turn off those sad love songs and instead listen to songs of praise and worship. When we praise God, we forget ourselves, and we open ourselves to His love. We need to get rid of everything that reminds us of the person who broke our heart, even if it's just for a while. We need to box all that stuff up and put it into the closet or throw it away—it makes no difference which, as long as we get it out of sight. When we feel we are starting to be overwhelmed by sad memories, we can turn on the TV, or we can call a friend to talk about anything other than the breakup, or, best of all, we can spend some time with Jesus.

If we feel as if all the couples in the world are being happy and loving just to make us miserable, we need to turn our heads—there is always another direction to look at. Most importantly, we need to stay busy. We can motivate ourselves to look better than ever, pamper ourselves, maybe join a gym. We can focus on school or on work, be ambitious, think about getting a promotion or a new job, earn a Master's degree or a PhD, or simply make it our goal to graduate with honors.

Do you see? It is up to us! We decide if we are going to collapse and let ourselves go, or if we are going to live through the disaster and succeed, no matter what. We are the ones who can consciously place ourselves in God's hands and allow Him to redirect our lives and heal our hearts. For us, there should be no other option but that we will live through it, we will help ourselves and we will be happy again!

Wisdom to contemplate:

"You are the salt of the earth. But if salt loses its taste, with what can it be seasoned? It is no longer good for anything but to be thrown out and trampled underfoot." (Mathew 5:13)

"You are the light of the world. A city set on a mountain cannot be hidden."(Mathew 5:14)

"So humble yourselves under the mighty hand of God, that he may exalt you in due time." (1 Peter 5:6)

"Humble yourselves before the Lord and he will exalt you." (James 4:10)

Set of Events
–29–

Ellie could not move. It was as if a huge weight was pinning her arms and legs down onto the bed. She could not scream. The only thing she could do was look around and blink. She was terrified. She could feel an awful presence in her room. What was it? Outside her closed bedroom door, she could hear what sounded like the awful growling of a furious dog. She could see what seemed like yellowish clouds that appeared and disappeared. She started praying to God: "Please, Jesus, help me. Jesus, please come and help me." Slowly, little by little, she started regaining movement in her hands, then her arms, then her feet and finally her legs. She was so scared she could not talk. She knew she had to take her car keys, run down the stairs and go out to the car. But would she be able to? She managed to draw some strength and courage, and she flew down the stairs, out the door and into her car. The night was calm and chilly. There was nobody around. It was 4:00 a.m., and people had yet to get up for their morning routine.

She sped away toward Jonah's house, which was on campus and which he shared with a couple of roommates. "It's OK," she thought. "His bed is next to the window, and I will be able to get his attention without waking the rest of the guys up." She parked and hurried to the side of the house where his bedroom was. She approached the window, which, as always, was open. “Jonah…Jonah,” she whispered, loud enough to wake him, but soft enough that she would not wake up the whole neighborhood.

It took a while, but he heard her and got up. She told him what had happened, and he believed her. It was not the first time eerie things had happened in that apartment. When he had been spending lots of time there, he had experienced many things himself. Besides, he knew Ellie was not the type of person to make something up just to get attention. He got dressed in a hurry, and they sped back to the apartment. Ellie wanted him to check every centimeter of it, and she asked him to stay with her until it was time to go to work.

“It is not the first time this has happened here, huh, Ellie!?” he said.

“No, and you know things only got worse after you left. A few times, for example, I have heard someone banging on the screen door, and when I looked through the window, there was nobody there. Other times, when the same thing happened, I asked loudly, “Who is there?” and nobody answered. It is very hard for me not to be terrified, and it is becoming almost impossible to live here!” She was obviously badly shaken. “One day, I came into the kitchen and felt a horrible pain in my foot—I was barefoot. When I looked down, there were maggots on the floor. They seemed to be coming from under the small kitchen rug. When I lifted it up, I almost had a heart attack—there were hundreds of filthy maggots furiously curling and twisting around. Can you believe it? A white chubby maggot had bitten me. He took a tiny chunk out of my foot. It is not normal, you know!"

The time came for Ellie to get ready to go to work, and Jonah gave her a big hug goodbye. Ellie went about her day as usual, but the experience stayed in the back of her mind.

"Mom, I am so glad you believe me. I thought you might tell me I am going crazy and need to go and look for help," Ellie said, relieved, when she talked to Anna on the phone that night.

"Ellie, you know that I know that you always tell me the truth. There is no chance in the world that I would doubt your word," Anna said lovingly. "I have heard many different theories about this kind of thing. The fact of the matter is— it doesn't matter. The reasons why you are having such experiences are not the important thing. The important thing is to find a solution, to find a way to make them stop. Look, Ellie, you have always been a very sensitive girl. Some people call it ESP, others call it mystical experiences, others something else—the name doesn't really matter. The point is that you might be more sensitive than usual because lately you have been very sad about the breakup with Jonah. Perhaps you are not as focused on where you want to be and on what you believe. Put your eyes on Jesus, Ellie. He has always been your strength and your rock. I know you believe in Him and in His loving protection. So, set your eyes on Jesus, don't forget to pray, and you will see that you will beat your fears, and your experiences will cease. I am sure. I promise you that!"

It was true. Anna was right. At first, when she and Jonah had just broken up, Ellie had drawn nearer to Jesus than she had ever been since she had been a teenager. But as soon as she had made up her mind that she was going to forget Jonah and try to be happy, she had focused so much on having friends, meeting people and having fun that she had neglected her relationship with God. She had been so busy being busy that she had almost forgotten about tending to her spiritual needs. She was always too tired to pray at night and would quickly fall asleep. She always had something to do on Sundays, so she frequently found herself saying, "I will go to church next Sunday."

She had been careless and slowly but surely had drifted away from Jesus and His loving arms. She was aware of this now and would immediately make the necessary changes in her life. God had always taken care of her and blessed her. She wondered how she could have stopped paying attention to Him. Before she knew it, she had been carried away by the current of everyday life into the world of carefree, superficial enjoyment. No more. She missed her beloved Jesus and having Him play an active part in her life. She would not neglect Him anymore. Deep down inside, she knew that the mediocrity of her spiritual life was the reason for all of her chilling experiences. She had let down her guard. She looked out her window towards the deep blue sky and thought about how this world can become a pretty scary place without the saving protection that a strong relationship with God brings. She turned on her iPod and listened to her favorite song. It went something like this: "Deliver me out of the sadness. Deliver me from all of the madness. Deliver me, Your courage to guide me. Deliver me, Your strength inside me." She made it her prayer that night.

Ellie was twenty-four years old.

Don't let your faith dwindle

The Bible tells us: "Faith is the realization of what is hoped for and evidence of things not seen."(Hebrews 11:1) What do we hope for? We hope for God's promises to become a reality in our lives. Faith believes these promises will be fulfilled. Faith is experiencing God's love, even though we might not see Him with our eyes. Faith is the glasses, placed on the eyes of our heart, through which we see God. Faith is a gift.

In the Bible, God also tells us: "The victory that conquers the world is our faith." (1 John 5:4) This is a huge statement to meditate on, because faith is something we should never take for granted.

Is our faith real, or is it a counterfeit? Does it arise out of the passing emotion of the moment, or is it everlasting? Is it there to stay, or will it be stolen by the enemy when trials, persecution or temptations come? In my opinion, a great benefit comes from second-guessing ourselves and not being too proud about the greatness of our faith. Why? We can become too excited and too overconfident, and then we will be in danger because this is when the enemy will attack us. Scripture says "Be sober and vigilant. Your opponent the devil is prowling around like a roaring lion looking for someone to devour. Resist him steadfast in faith..."(1 Peter 5:8-9) Faith is a shield, and so we must always have our shield up and ready—but if we are overconfident, we might not realize our shield is not as strong as it needs to be! We do not want to get too comfortable and let down our guard. Hence we must give our hearts and elevate our minds to God each morning, surrendering our will and placing our trust in Him, humbly asking Him to strengthen our faith.

How can we believe in someone we do not see? God is so good and loving to His children that He has revealed Himself to us. All we need to do is to want to get to know Him. It is difficult to believe in Someone we do not personally know, to believe in that Person's goodness, love, mercy and power. If we say we have faith in God, but we have not taken the time to get to know Him, this could mislead us—we might end up thinking it is enough to just say we have faith.

Saying we have faith is not enough. It does not necessarily mean we have faith in our hearts. We might want to have faith, might even try to have faith, but without getting to know God, our efforts are in vain. Knowing requires learning. I know math only after I learn math. Likewise, I know my classmates only after I take time to learn about who they are and what is going on in their lives.

In the same way, learning about God can lead us to knowing God. And knowing God will lead us to loving God, and loving God will lead us to having great faith and trust in Him. Why? Because, as we fall in love with Him, we will naturally desire to do His will. As we start to do His will, our life will be turned around, and His graces will fully flow into our heart. Faith, God's greatest gift to us, will then become firmly established in us, and we will be able to see the difference that it makes to live our lives in the presence of God.

As we get to know God, a great desire to love Him will be unleashed. As we come to understand the greatness of His love for us and see how He loved us first, we will desperately try to love Him back, and then we will quickly come to the realization that to love Him we need to align ourselves with His will. This takes work. We cannot just lean back and say, "I believe in God, and this is enough for me." No way! We need to put time into our relationship with Him. Only then will we come to experience the fullness of His promises. Only then will we come to enjoy the fruits of His Spirit living in us. Only then will we come to live under the shadow of His wings.

When we get to know God, we learn that we need to follow His ways in order to be fulfilled in this world and completely happy in the next. We cannot just try to do it our way! He is all knowing, and we are not, so we need to listen to Him and do what He tells us! Through prayer, meditation and Bible reading, we come to understand what He wants from us. If we are humble and we recognize that there is much for us to learn and much for us to change, we will allow His loving hands to mold us and make us brand new. Then we will start experiencing a brand new life.

We must make a commitment to learn His ways, doing what He tells us, obeying His loving words of advice for us. Like the psalmist, we need to pray: "Your word is a lamp for my feet, a light for my path. I make a solemn vow to keep your just edicts…Your decrees are my heritage forever; they are the joy of my heart. My heart is set on fulfilling your laws; they are my reward forever." (Psalm 119:105-106,111-112) This psalm reflects a true understanding of the fact that God loves us with an everlasting perfect love. All He wants is for us is to be safe under the shadow of His protection. His desire for us is for us to experience the joy that it is to have His love living inside our hearts. His desire for us is for us to come to everlasting life.

We must take to heart words of advice that have been said by Christians before us. Great saints give great advice. I once read that "In the deepest solitude, God speaks to our hearts." Maybe that is why sometimes He allows us to become a bit lonely, so that we can let go of all that is preventing us from listening to Him. Only then, when we are ready to listen, can He lovingly speak to our hearts and show us the way to be followed.

Faith makes us act. If faith does not make us act, then we have fooled ourselves, and perhaps we have no faith at all. As it says in the book of James,

faith without actions is dead. (James 2:17) And faith that is dead is no faith at all. True faith saves us because it leads us to go to Him and to follow Him with our hearts and with our actions. Have we come to know God yet? What are we waiting for?!

Wisdom to contemplate:

"But without faith it is impossible to please him, for anyone who approaches God must believe that he exists and that he rewards those who seek him." (Hebrews 11:6)

"For by grace you have been saved through faith, and this is not from you; it is the gift of God." (Ephesians 2:8)

"No trial has come to you but what is human. God is faithful and will not let you be tried beyond your strength; but with the trial he will also provide a way out, so that you may be able to bear it." (1 Corinthians 10:13)

"For we walk by faith, not by sight" (2 Corinthians 5:7)

"Jesus said to him, '"If you can!" Everything is possible to one who has faith.' Then the boy's father cried out, 'I do believe, help my unbelief!'"
(Mark 9:23-24)

"Do not let your hearts be troubled. You have faith in God; have faith also in me." (John 14:1)

Angel
–30–

It was Easter Sunday. Ellie's friend Andy had called her to ask her out. She had woken up thinking about Jonah, and she could not get him out of her mind. She told Andy how she felt and how she had dated so many guys to forget him—in vain. She told him that the more she dated the more she missed Jonah and that she was sure Jonah was the one, the love of her life.

"So call him, my friend," Andy replied. "What are you waiting for? Call him right now and tell him everything you just told me. Tell him that you want to make things right."

"I can't call him," Ellie said. "He hurt my feelings. He just left me when things got tough. He broke my heart. I can never trust him again."

But Ellie could not stop thinking about what Andy had said. So she decided to call Anna.

"Look, Ellie. Do you know what is the greatest obstacle between people and their happiness? It is their ego. You have to get rid of your ego for the sake of your happiness. Pride in this moment serves no good purpose. You want to be happy, and you believe that he is the one. You said yourself that he is about to move to another state to do his Master's degree. So, if you do not take a chance now, you might lose your

chance forever. Many times opportunities pass in front of us only once. We have to grab them because if we let them go by, we might be missing that chance forever. We need to seize the day—tomorrow things might not be the same. Call while it is still today."

Anna waited for a response, any response. Ellie told her that she needed time to think about it all and hung up.

Ellie was thoughtful. She respected Andy's opinion very much. On top of everything, now Anna agreed with him. Her mom had always been right when it came to giving her advice. And Andy had been a good friend, actually more than that—he had been like an angel to her when she needed someone the most.

"OK," she said. "I'll call him."

Ellie had called Andy back and was carefully listening to him. "Now, Ellie," he said. "Call him now! If not, you will lose the momentum. Go with the power of the moment. Sounds funky, huh! Look. Just call right away. Promise me, right now, that as soon as we hang up, you will call him." Andy's voice was full of excitement with a touch of authority.

"I promise," Ellie said hesitantly.

She was nervous. What if Jonah didn't want anything to do with her anymore? What if…? What if…? Fear of rejection was making Ellie freeze at the thought of dialing the number.

“Hello.” She heard Jonah’s answer on the other end of the line.

“It’s me,” Ellie said fearfully. She told him she needed to see him.

It took a little convincing, but soon afterward Jonah was pulling up in front of her door. There they were, the black car and the white car, next to each other again. How much she had missed that, such a simple thing that had made her heart ache so many times. He knocked on the door and came in.

She told him how she felt when she had dated other people and how, no matter how many things had happened, she was sure that he was the one and they could work things out. She just needed to find out if he felt the same way.

He told her he loved her. Of course, he loved her. And he had missed her so much. As soon as he had left her door the day they broke up, he had understood immediately that he had made the biggest mistake of his life. That summer, he had been miserable and so sad that he had gotten sick. He had not been able to eat anything without throwing up. He had regretted everything the moment he realized he would have to start his life over without her. He had missed her laugh, her company, her warmth—the list was endless. Nobody could take her place. He had known she was the one from the moment he had first seen her. He was so sorry, and he felt so lucky to have her in front of him, telling him these things.

"Look, it is Easter," she said with a smile. "Would you come to Easter Sunday mass with me?"

They got into his car and headed toward the church, full of dreams, full of hope.

Let's be angels to each other

So many people nowadays believe in angels, in interacting with them, seeking their help, trying to talk to them, trying to see them. But today there is also much confusion about angels, because the secular view of angels has invaded the media. There are books, films, songs—you name it—about angels. A lot of people have become obsessed with angels and have become insensitive to their friends, coworkers, neighbors and even family members. In their pursuit of angels, they have forgotten the most important thing: giving praise and glory to God by loving one another. They are so busy trying to interact with an angel that they lose touch with their personal relationship with others and many times even with God. Now, I am going to propose another view on angels.

I am not saying angels don't exist or that they are not important—please don't get me wrong. What I have a problem with is when people's obsession with angels makes them overlook the teachings of Jesus Christ and leads them to neglect their relationship with God. Once Jesus Christ is a priority in our lives, we can then learn to love and respect the angels.

Why do we obsess about angels? I think because we crave a stronger, more solid relationship with God. We want to be more spiritual, but we approach it in a proud and even selfish way: "I and my angel", "I have a unique relationship with angels", "I am special because I communicate with angels", "I am unique and good because I see my guardian angel." In the end, we might end up forgetting others. We can become so focused on ourselves that we forget the main thing God wants us to do—which is to love one another and take care of each other. Jesus Christ left us a message about loving one another. If we can focus on this, then we can be like living, breathing angels to each other. The message of Jesus was a powerful message of love in every sense of the word—love in the sense of giving without expecting back, forgiving, not judging, treating others as we would like to be treated, helping those who are different, helping those who are in need, helping the sad, the lonely and the hungry.

We can be angels to each other. We can give more time to others. We can listen to them, offer them our company, give them our support. We can be more patient with each other and more kind. We can change the world with our love, moving forward step by step, without having any grandiose expectations of "becoming enlightened" or "interacting with angels."

We can be content to just be ourselves, a simple person with many defects but capable of loving all the same. Knowing deep in our hearts that we are a unique child of God made in His image to love and to be loved.

Jesus came so that we would become children of God. Why do people get lost and start almost worshiping angels, obsessing about them...and all the while neglecting their relationship with God? All we need to say is: "God, Father, I need help," and He will immediately send His angels so that we won't even hit our foot against a stone. (Psalm 91:12) When we trust God and ask for His help, we know that His help will come—through His angels in heaven or through those people who, out of love, become, even if for a moment, angels on earth.

Wisdom to contemplate:

"Let love be sincere; hate what is evil, hold on to what is good; love one another with mutual affection; anticipate one another in showing honor. Do not grow slack in zeal, be fervent in spirit, serve the Lord. Rejoice in hope, endure in affliction, persevere in prayer. Contribute to the needs of the holy ones, exercise hospitality. Bless those who persecute (you), bless and do not curse them. Rejoice with those who rejoice, weep with those who weep. Have the same regard for one another; do not be haughty but associate with the lowly; do not be wise in your own estimation. Do not repay anyone evil for evil; be concerned for what is noble in the sight of all. If possible, on your part, live at peace with all. Beloved, do not look for revenge but leave room for the wrath; for it is written, 'Vengeance is mine, I will repay, says the Lord.' Rather, 'if your enemy is hungry, feed him; if he is thirsty, give him something to drink; for by so doing you will heap burning coals upon his head.' Do not be conquered by evil but conquer evil with good. (Romans 12:9-21)

Together Again
–31–

They were together in church, attending Easter Sunday mass. As they sat next to each other, Ellie prayed to God and asked for His blessing. She prayed that she and Jonah would fix their problems and be together again…this time forever. She was completely into her prayer when she felt his hand gently holding hers. She opened her eyes, and he was looking at her. He smiled and pressed her hand with his. She knew her prayer had been answered.

After mass, they headed home because there was much to talk about. There was still a lot that they needed to clear up. She told him that she had reconsidered and that she could move to his country and give it a try. She had had a lot of time to think about this, and she had realized that she had been wrong. Why close the door on such an opportunity? Why shut out the possibility of being happy together somewhere else? After all, her whole life she had moved from place to place. Nothing would be different this time, except that she would be starting a new life with the love of her life.

"Look, there is only one thing I need to know for sure, and that is that I will be able to see my parents at least once a year," Ellie said. "As long as I can visit my family often, I have no problem with moving away."

"Of course, Ellie. I know how important your family is to you!" Jonah answered, full of love.

Ellie told him that she would leave the baby issue in the hands of God. She knew that if a baby was in God's plan, Jonah would one day change his mind. She knew that God had picked Jonah for her, that he was the guy that she was meant to spend the rest of her life with. Yes, she was sure that he was the prince she had prayed for when she was little. She knew this, and so she let herself be solely governed by her faith.

Ellie told Jonah that there was only one thing in which she could not give in. Either they knew they loved each other, or it was time to say goodbye. She would not live together with him, and she would not go into a never-ending dating relationship. That just seemed pointless. It was time to make a decision. If they were to stay together, they would do it the right way. They would get married.

Jonah agreed. Actually, he wanted to go the airport and fly to Las Vegas to get married that same night. Ellie said no way. This time, they would do it the way she had always dreamed— in the church with God's blessing of course, big wedding, long white dress, three-tiered cake, the whole nine yards! She wanted it all or nothing.

Jonah told her she was going to be his princess from that day on…and that he would make it his mission to make all of her dreams come true.

Ellie had placed her life in the hands of God. She knew that this time it would be different. She closed her eyes and thanked God.

And so came the day Ellie had been dreaming of. Jonah was looking very handsome in a black tuxedo with a burgundy belt and a burgundy tie as he entered the church next to his mother. The small chapel was full of candles and peach-colored roses. It was better than the picture perfect wedding Ellie had dreamed of when she was a little girl.

Ellie was in a gorgeous gown, slightly off her shoulders, with small beige roses on the sleeves. She had a long veil that had tiny pearls sewn onto it. She was a beautiful bride. The wedding march started playing, with violins and a flute, and she slowly started approaching the altar, holding Reuben's arm.

Reuben looked at Ellie and smiled. He knew his daughter had found happiness. A tear escaped his eye. He was happy…he was sad. His Ellie was now a woman. He was about to give her away to her future husband, and a new chapter in her life was just starting.

Anna was looking at Ellie with joy. "Look at my little girl," she told herself. "She makes such a beautiful bride." She closed her eyes and thanked God.

Ellie took a big breath, closed her eyes and also thanked God. One more time, He had turned things around in her life. One more time, He had answered her prayers. A deep feeling of gratefulness invaded her heart.

Ellie was now twenty-five years old.

The power of forgiveness

Yes! I have left forgiveness for the last chapter! In a way, I have left the best for last. Forgiveness is a key ingredient we need in our quest for happiness. Without forgiveness, we are lost. Let me explain why: To love is to forgive. To forgive is to love. And to love is the most important thing in the world!

Can we forgive? Can we give a second chance to someone whom we once loved but who has hurt us deeply in some way? Can we bury the past and find the love and the strength to start again? Is this possible? Can we trust again? Can we get rid of the fear of getting hurt again? Is it possible to let down our guard, once more becoming vulnerable to a person who has hurt us deeply?

To forgive is hard, but it is not impossible. To forgive is a choice we make, and, like every other choice, it involves risks. But the higher the risk factor the higher the profit—this is what they say in the business world, but it is also true in life. How, you may wonder, do we stand to profit? Ah! We will profit in every way. In forgiving, we give one more chance to that person who has hurt us. But, in giving a second chance to the person who has hurt us, in a way we are giving a second chance to ourselves! We all are humans. We all have fears and complexes. None of us is perfect. We all make mistakes. So, then, we should always be ready to forgive others. You may say that it is easier said than done. True, but good things don't come easily.

Forgiveness is possible if we bury the past. If we keep bringing up the past, then forgiveness can't happen. We cannot heal a wound we keep picking at! A wound needs to be left alone, to allow it to heal. Many times, forgiving is the difference between happiness and unhappiness. But we cannot do it on our own. The Bible says that we can do all things through Jesus Christ, who strengthens us. (Philippians 4:13) We might feel that we do not have the strength, but God can give us the strength. We might feel that we are too scared, but God will give us peace. We might feel that we have too much anger, but God will replace the anger with love. We might think that we will never be able to forget, but God will keep us busy with joyful new moments, so that we can leave the sorrow in the past.

There is only one thing God wants us to do, and that is to put our ego aside. There is no room for ego in love. Our ego must diminish if our love is to increase. So, if someone you love deeply has hurt you, and this person is asking for a second chance, open your heart and take a chance. It may be the best decision you ever made. After all, the best thing we can do so that our lives are better is to follow God's advice—and He is big on forgiveness! He says: "Put on then, as God's chosen ones, holy and beloved, heartfelt compassion, kindness, humility, gentleness, and patience, bearing with one another and forgiving one another, if one has a grievance against another; as the Lord has forgiven you, so must you also do. And over all these put on love, that is, the bond of perfection. And let the peace of Christ control your hearts, the peace into which you were also called in one body. And be thankful." (Colossians 3:12-15)

Let love reign in your life. Let God show you how!

Wisdom to contemplate:

"When you stand to pray, forgive anyone against whom you have a grievance, so that your heavenly Father may in turn forgive you your transgressions." (Mark 11:25)

"If your brother sins, rebuke him; and if he repents, forgive him. And if he wrongs you seven times in one day and returns to you seven times saying, 'I am sorry,' you should forgive him." (Luke 17:3-4)

"Be merciful, just as (also) your Father is merciful. Stop judging and you will not be judged. Stop condemning and you will not be condemned. Forgive and you will be forgiven. Give and gifts will be given to you; a good measure, packed together, shaken down, and overflowing, will be poured into your lap. For the measure with which you measure will in return be measured out to you." (Luke 6:36-38)

Made in the USA
Charleston, SC
28 November 2014